CULTURAL HERITAGE AND CONTEMPORARY CHANGE
SERIES IV, WEST EUROPE, VOLUME 3
*General Editor*
*George F. McLean*



# Italy at the Millennium:
## Economy, Politics, Literature and Journalism

***The 1999 Edmund D. Pellegrino Lectures on Contemporary Italian Politics***

Edited by
*PAOLO JANNI*

*Department of Politics, The Catholic University of America*
*The Council for Research in Values and Philosophy*

Box 261
Cardinal Station
Washington, D.C. 20064


Printed in the United States of America

**Library of Congress Cataloging-in-Publication**

Italy at the millennium: economy, politics, literature and journalism: the 1999 Edmund D. Pellegrino lectures on contemporary Italian politics / edited by Paolo Janni.

p. cm. — (Cultural heritage and contemporary change. Series IV, Western Europe; vol. 3)

Includes bibliographical references and index.

1. Italy -- Economic conditions -- 20th century.
2. Italy -- Politics and government -- 20th century.
3. Literature and Society.
4. Jounalism -- Italy.

I. Janni, Polo. II. Series.

HC305 .I793 2001
330.945'093--dc21 2001000860
CIP

ISBN 1-56518-158-1 (pbk.)

## CONTENTS

*Introduction* 1

Chapter I. The Presidency in Transition: Constitution and Praxis in Italy 7
*Maria Elisabetta de Franciscis*

Chapter II. Literature and Society in Italy 69
*Maristella de Panizza Lorch*

Chapter III. The Italian Economy Facing the Euro-Challenge 113
*Giannandrea Falchi*

Chapter IV. WUI: Writing under the Influence: Journalism and Power in Post-War Italy 123
*Vittorio Zucconi*

*About the Authors* 149

*Index* 151

# INTRODUCTION

In 1999 Prime Minister D'Alema failed to control and keep together the ramshackle coalition of parties which supported his government. The deep splits in the ranks were fueled by his former Christian Democrat allies. They had not forgiven him for the removal from office of their man and the winner of the 1996 election, Romano Prodi. D'Alema's qualities as a master political tactician did not save him from the humiliations that the internal squabbles of the coalition almost daily inflicted upon him. The divisions inside his government sapped confidence in his ability to advance his program. D'Alema's party, the Democrats of the Left, lost ground in the June elections for the European Parliament; they lost as well the election for the renewal of the city council of Bologna, a communist stronghold for 54 years. Meanwhile, the opposition *Forza Italia* of media tycoon Silvio Berlusconi emerged as the largest national party.

Carlo Azeglio Ciampi was elected President of the Republic by the Italian parliament on the first ballot, with well over two thirds of the required majority., He was widely respected as former Governor of the Bank of Italy and former Prime Minister, who more than anyone else helped bring the Lira into Europe's single currency and Italy into the European Monetary System. Most Italians rely now on his skills and nonpartisan approach to move domestically toward a more stable and efficient political system. At the European level they depend on him to strengthen Italy's role in making "Europe's political stage coincide with its geographic borders", as he said in his acceptance speech on May 18, 1999.

Two separate courts, one in Palermo and another in Perugia, cleared Giulio Andreotti — the longest serving Italian politician, statesman, and an icon of the post WWII Italian political landscape — of the accusation of being the Mafia's chief protector and of any involvement in the death of an Italian journalist. Both acquittals have vindicated in some way all former Christian Democrats, many of whom had been humiliated and politically destroyed by the wave of judicial inquires called *"Mani Pulite"* or clean hands. Andreotti has started making his political voice heard again from his stall as "Senator for Life".

The year 1999 also saw Italy fully engaged in its biggest humanitarian effort for the refugees fleeing Albania and later in the NATO air strikes against Yugoslavia to "halt the genocide in progress in Kosovo", as Prime Minister D'Alema said. Italy provided 11 airfields for NATO's airflights, 5000 ground troops in Macedonia and Albania for the peacekeeping mission in Kosovo and more than two hundred paramilitary police. Moreover, thousands of Italian civilian volunteers assisted tens of thousands of displaced persons in that area, with the full support of Italian public opinion.

But the most urgent domestic questions — from the reform of the electoral system to how to face the massive influx of illegal immigrants — are still there and remain unanswered: corruption still pervades society; the percentage of young people unemployed is still very high; Unions have problems adopting a *modus operandi* more consistent with the reality of an open and competitive economy; the banking system seems more interested in mergers or takeovers than in providing efficient services at competitive costs; the economic system as a whole still seeks old fashioned forms of subsidies and political patronage, despite its noisy rhetoric over the virtues of the market.

Against this background, both political blocs — the center left and the center right — seem more busy with their own survival than in dealing with the country's affairs. Both are made up of a rainbow of very different political expressions kept together by their desire to keep or to go back to power. Both try to gain electoral favors more from the mistakes of the other than by advancing realistic proposals on how to overcome the country's difficulties. None of them has a culture of bipartisan approach to Italy's problems.

Rather than "leaders" they are both "followers" of the public mood and none has yet offered a vision of the kind of Italian political society they are proposing. In the pre-electoral stage Italians know more what the competing and heterogeneous political blocks are against than what they are for.

The present volume records the four lectures given in 1999 by Maria Elisabetta de Franciscis, Maristella de Panizza Lorch, Giannandrea Falchi and Vittorio Zucconi in the framework of "The Edmund D. Pellegrino Series of Lectures on Italian Politics". The program was initiated in 1997 with the full support of the Department of Politics of the Catholic University of America and is now in its third year.

In "*The Presidency: Constitution and Praxis in Italy*" Maria Elisabetta de Franciscis extensively analyses the powers of the President of the Republic as enumerated in the Constitution. She analyzes as well the role and functions of the President throughout the last fifteen years. Her attempt is to evaluate if the President have slowly moved away from the roles of representative of national unity and guarantor of the constitutional order to that of an actor upon the political scene.

The hypothesis explored by de Franciscis is that from the tenure of Einaudi to that of Scalfaro, a presidential praxis has developed affecting the Presidency more than any other constitutional order through an "enigmatic accumulation of non homogenous powers".

She looks at the powers of the Presidency in a country which has chosen the parliamentary form of government with the legislative branch being the most important of the three branches and the main agent in Italian political life. Nevertheless this system has developed in the last fifteen years along pathological lines, attributing too much power to the political parties. As a consequence the most important decisions gradually have been taken outside the Parliament, slowly transforming the latter into a passive legislature.

Moreover, she argues, throughout the last decade the Italian people have experienced a sudden awakening of previously dormant democratic and moralistic sentiments, while discovering a keenness for efficiency and parliamentary productivity. The last fifty years have been marked by participatory democracy, schooling and higher education, and exposure to media and other information tools. A majority of Italians — older and younger, from the north as well as from the south — have come to appreciate the potentialities of the fundamental Law. At the same time, they have ceased to ignore the deficiencies and the pathological evolution of some institutions.

Hence one speaks of a "transition," but not in the sense of its common definition, for it should have embraced a much shorter period of time than over fifteen years of the evolution of the presidential powers. Neither does it seem appropriate to define this period as a "transitory regime," for that would require a clear date for its initiation and for its termination. Rather we now experience a change which slowly is moving the nation away from the rigid enumeration and separation of powers, typical of Civil Law countries. Instead, we are drawing closer to the Common Law countries where there are more possibilities of two branches acting in the same areas. There the elasticity of interpretation allows for a pendulum-like alternation of forces accepted even by the highest courts as a natural contribution to the making of a mature democracy.

We are in the presence of a new balance between the President of the Republic and Parliament in a system in which the President has acquired political powers and must now be considered an active and vital member of the executive branch. The fact that during the first months of the mandate of president Ciampi there has been a return to article 138 of the Constitution may be seen, not as the President of the Republic being remiss or trying to guarantee the 1948 constitutional order, but rather as a "return" of the *pendulum* in favor of the Parliament, typical of a Common Law system. We could be in the presence of yet another element in favor of the theory of "cross-fertilization", which has revealed a convergence, neither intentional nor conscious, of the main juridical families.

Maristella de Panizza Lorch deals with the complex relations between *"Literature and Society in Italy"*. The initial part of her essay points to Dante and Ariosto, whose poems offer two paradigmatic examples of an ideal relationship of literature to society. It notes as well the Renaissance humanism of Ariosto's *Orlando Furioso* which, she notes, acquires a lightness of language often in wake of Dante's weight.

The second section is dedicated to literature and society in contemporary Italy. Lorch singles out a novel (Alberto Arbasino's *Fratelli d'Italia*) and reviews the main authors who have contributed to a special kind of detective novel called "il giallo", the noir. The third part of her lecture relates extensively to the "Debates' which took place in Italian literature from 1945 to now.

Finally she outlines a special profile of Leonardo Sciascia and for two reasons. First, because his life stretches through Fascism and the war to the post war moment of ecstasy when writers believed they could write as The Voice of the People. Sciascia, she notes, takes part in the intense literary debates of the avant-guard in the sixties, but at a distance and from the advantage point of his insular balcony. In the seventies and the eighties, however, he dives ferociously into the accusation of political power. Second, because of his marvelous combination of cold irony and warm passion, the harmonious coexistence of reason and non reason, the passion with which he embraces an idea lives with it. He works around it in his own mind until finally he translates it into a most concise written form.

The structural problems still affecting the Italian economy and the financial system eleven months after the European Monetary System came into force are dealt with by Giannandrea Falchi in the chapter on "*The Italian Economy Facing the Euro Challenge*".

An uncertain growth perspective, he argues, coupled with an aging population (18 percent is over the age of 65) has diminished the propensity to invest. Moreover, the industrial sector is characterized by a middle technology, the fiscal burden remains high and a few bottlenecks in the labor market still impede the proper allocation of human resources.

On a more positive side, the public sector deficit, which declined from 9.2 percent of GDP in 1994 to 2.7 percent in 1998, should be around 2.2 percent this year. The Italian banking and financial system has become more integrated into the global economy, although there is still a gap when compared with other industrialized countries. A bolder expansion of the stock market is limited by the low propensity of medium to larger sized business to become listed and by the number of small businesses that do not resort to the market. Moreover, direct investments abroad by Italian companies grows more than the investment in Italy by non-residents. Therefore the ability to attract investors in Italy must be reinforced.

For most of the '90s Italy's economy had been driven by two external forces: Europe and the market. Political pressure was brought by the deadlines and conditions of the European Monetary

Union, together with economic pressure consisting of the international financial markets' continuous judgment of Italy's ability to meet EMU membership criteria. Today Italy faces new challenges which generate internally the same kind of catalyst which permitted its entry in the Euro, and the solving of its remaining structural problems.

Finally, in his provocative and irreverent essay, *"Writing Under the Influence: Journalism and Power in Post-War Italy,"* Vittorio Zucconi argues that to be a journalist in Italy — and to some extent in Europe — is to swim against the current of a tradition that has never seen the kind of unabridged freedom and independence taken for granted in the United States.

When journalism is bad, as now it so often is, in Italy we have a few little alibis to hide behind. In the United States when journalism is bad the news people have no one to blame but themselves. Nevertheless, he adds, the gap between the "Italian way" and the "American way" has narrowed dramatically since the beginning of the 80s.

The influences under which Italian journalists write originate both from within and from without. None is more insidious and pervasive than the deeply rooted Italian conviction that power is dangerous, must be tamed and, most of all, shared. The immediate post WWII, with all its apparent new found freedom, did nothing to change an approach that had matured through generations.

My warm thanks go to Dr. David Walsh, Acting Chairman of the Department of Politics of the Catholic University of America, and Dr. Stephen Schneck for their strong support of the program. I wish also to express my special gratitude to George F. McLean, Professor Emeritus of Philosophy and Executive Secretary of the Council for Research in Values and Philosophy for bearing with me. This publication has been possible only trough his good will, his advise, and his endless Christian patience.

*Paolo Janni*
Senior Fellow in European Politics
The Catholic University of America Washington D.C
November 2000

# CHAPTER I

# THE PRESIDENCY IN TRANSITION: CONSTITUTION AND PRAXIS IN ITALY

*MARIA ELISABETTA DE FRANCISCIS*

Table of Contents: 1. Premises; 2. Historic Background; 3. The 1948 Constitution; 4. The Transition; 5. The Presidency; 6. The Powers of the President; 7. The Presidency in Transition; 8. Developments; 9. Conclusions.

## PREMISES

To those who are not familiar with contemporary Italian politics or government, the title given to this lecture may appear both misleading and contradictory. At the present time, in fact, Italy has a parliamentary government.[1] Even in the extremely chaotic and confusing political environment which Italy has enjoyed since the end of World War II, a *datum*, which can hardly be unproven, is the fact that Italy has chosen and has maintained the parliamentary form of government. This implies that, of the three branches of government, the most important is the legislative branch.[2] It is this branch indeed, which is the depositary of the people's sovereignty, and, it is this branch which will pass a vote of confidence on the President of the Council of ministers and to the Cabinet as a whole.[3] Likewise, it is an understatement to affirm that the Italian parliamentary system has developed along pathological lines, attributing too much power to political parties[4] which, in order to maintain their control, concentrated all decision making to the highest levels, slowly transforming Parliament into a passive legislator. It is in this institutional vacuum that the Presidents of the Republic have found the opportunity to enlarge their sphere of influence, thus transforming the presidency. It is appropriate, therefore, rather than odd, to look at the powers and the role of the President of the Republic in a country which has chosen the parliamentary form of government.

It is unquestionable that the 1948 constitution was one

which represented of the historic period in which it was drafted. The Presidency, as every other fundamental aspect of the constitution, such as regionalism, parliamentary government and multipartitism, is a blend of reactions to the authoritative government of Mussolini and to continuity with the pre-fascist evolution of the early constitutional monarchy, which, from 1848, had been developing until it abruptly interrupted in 1922 by the *coup d'état.*

Likewise, it is no secret that, for the last 15 years, Italy has been undergoing drastic transformations moving both towards a new form of government and a new form of state. The changes which have occurred are fundamental not just because the relationship between the government and the people has changed,[5] but because these imply a much wider transformation.[6] It is likewise true that Italy does not follow the "pure" parliamentary model, and it is this "mixed" form, along with its pathological development, which has set in motion the constitutional transition known as the "peaceful revolution" of Italy.

The role and powers of the Head of State followed the same pattern. Articles 83 through 91 discipline and sanction a particular kind of Head of State. (**Table 1**) In fact, he is at the same time the heir of the old monarchy and the guarantor of the new system. He was considered by the constituent assembly a "neutral" power, that is, he was supposed to make sure that all of the constitutional branches of the new Republican government execute correctly their charges while avoiding taking an active role. Along with the Supreme Court of Italy, the President of the Republic was supposed to be then the highest and last magistrate of the country.

If this was the acclaimed position of the President of the Republic, how then, can we affirm that the President is the ideal figure to study in order to evaluate the length and depth of the transition Italy has been undergoing?.

The hypothesis of this paper is that the transition of the presidency, which is evident especially in the sphere of the powers of *stimulus*, has modified the most important functions attributed to the President of the Republic, converting him to an "actor" in the change, rather than keeping him as the guarantor of the respect of the constitutional order.

The contention is that Italy is very slowly, but certainly,

changing from a world of *civil law* to a world of *common law*. This transformation, which is not only the desire nor the platform of a specific government, seems to be an unconscious development, encouraged by fundamental modifications in the European Union.[7] If all of the above is true, the next drafting of a constitution by a Constituent Assembly or by a Bicameral Committee will be unable to start from the letter of the 1948 constitution, but will have to register what in *civil law* countries is called material constitution. In order to allow those who are not familiar with the Italian system to appreciate the transformations which are taking place in this country, it seems appropriate to begin with a brief historic background of the powers of the Head of State before and during the authoritative regime. This will be followed by a description of the intentions of the Constituent Assembly and of the "established" doctrine through the 1980s. An in-depth analysis of each of the presidential powers as it has been modified from the 1980s onwards will then follow.

## HISTORIC BACKGROUND

The 1848 constitution, known as the "Albertine Statute", has been erroneously considered an *octroyée* constitution, that is to say, that it was considered a constitution granted by the king to the people. As has been clearly demonstrated[8] and as is also more befitting the drafting of any fundamental law establishing progress in the field of human rights and liberties, the "Albertine Statute" is a compromise between a king who felt threatened and a new, up and coming *bourgeoisie*. It included all those powers and liberties, which the king perceived as not menacing to his own powers. It was indeed a typical reaction of the absolute monarch in order to maintain as much power as possible.

The Statute included provisions to introduce a constitutional monarchy.[9] The king was the head of state[10] and, in many ways, also the main lawmaker, although in 1848 a legislative branch was provided for.[11] He represented the nation. He was the sole person to which the executive powers were bestowed; He was Commander in Chief of the armed forces and declared war; He accredited and received diplomats; He signed international agreements;[12] He appointed all state officials;[13] He set the agenda for the Chambers and convened them, in addition to determining the dates for the election;[14] He gave royal assent to the laws and made sure that these laws were enforced;[15] He granted pardons and commuted punishments.[16]

The introduction of a new electoral law in 1912 can be considered the most important factor leading the country from an absolute to a constitutional monarchy and, eventually, to a parliamentary regime. It is through the latter,[17] the enlargement of the suffrage,[18] and the abolition of the *non expedit*[19] that more and more people are called to express their choice of representation while the legislative branch becomes stronger and the king weaker. Thus Parliament becomes truly representative of the people; the Cabinet itself drastically changes its constitutional role from the King's Cabinet to the House's Cabinet.

All of these changes, which were affected by the electoral law, did not imply constitutional amendments. The lack of the latter is what has misled many scholars in saying that Italy has had only two constitutions. A correct interpretation of constitutional history, instead, must lead to the conclusion that Italy has had at least four different constitutional regimes. Two of these revisions occurred before the advent of the dictatorship, one took place during the dictatorship itself, and the last one from 1948 to the present-day.[20]

## THE 1948 CONSTITUTION

The relationship between the executive and legislative branches of government sanctioned in the Constitution[21] allows the observer to define Italy as a parliamentary republic. The executive, in fact, depends on a vote of confidence by each of the two branches of Parliament, in order to be invested in the powers of the office. The constituent assembly meant for the Council of Ministers to be "responsible" to Parliament[22] not "dependent" on its vote, albeit it did not secure completely the stability of the German *Grundgesetz* of 1949, where a clause providing for a constructive vote of no confidence was included.[23]

The only guarantee for stability sanctioned in Article 94 of the Italian constitution is the provision that "*an opposing vote by one or both the Houses against a government proposal does not entail the obligation to resign.*" Yet, since 1948, all government crises but one[24] have been generated by a parliamentary defeat of a government proposal rather then by a motion of no confidence which would have had to "*be signed by at least one tenth of the members of the House.*"[25] Immediately after the expression of such a vote by either House, the President of the Council of ministers would resign his mandate to the President of the Republic, thus initiating a crisis. The "extra-parliamentary" government crisis, not foreseen by the Constituent Assembly, became the custom because of the political fragmentation of the legislative assemblies (due to the proportional electoral law), which, in turn, strengthened the already strong political parties[26] and appeared to weaken the role of the President of the Republic.

## THE TRANSITION

Time and again during the last twenty years, the various political forces have been debating on the need for reforms, postponing however, the actual implementation of them until just recently, when, more by the "force" of direct democracy (*referenda*) than by their political foresight, changes, at times radical, have begun to occur. The first one of these was the delegation of more powers, especially in the realm of fiscal autonomy, to the smallest of the administrative territorial subdivisions of Italy, the towns. With it, or as a consequence of it, came the new electoral law for mayors and town councilmen. Then the popular *referendum* of 1993, with which Parliamentarians received the moral mandate to rewrite the national election law from proportional to majoritarian, drastically reduced the role and the power which political parties had been enjoying since the 1946 Constituent Assembly. From these initial successes derived the complete turnover in both Houses of Parliament. In fact, most of the 945 elected legislators who took office in 1994 were freshmen who were to begin to look more seriously to the necessity of implementing sections of the fundamental law, which had been ignored and/or only partially and pathologically executed, and to revise entire segments of it in order to improve its standing with the people.

Among the reforms which have taken place since then, there are major laws and some constitutional amendments.

Executive efficiency and a more active role for Parliament were two rather conflicting objectives of the reforms. The procedures to accomplish such goals could have most likely varied due to reforms which each carried. Furthermore, the unfulfilled articles on decentralization[27] and the growing economic division between the northern and the southern parts of the country, coupled with the pressure brought upon the nation by the Maastricht Agreements, have generated the opinion that high levels of decentralization, or the Scottish model of devolution, could be the *panacea* for all the miss workings on the system. It seemed all too natural, then, that various proposals came under consideration during the XIIIth Legislature[28] and it would have seemed feasible for Parliament to satisfy all or some of the desires of the people.

Two levels of confrontation could be found, therefore, in Italy. The first one, more politically oriented, was focused on increasing the efficiency of the governmental system; the second one, more legally oriented, focused on the procedures to be followed in order to obtain the desired reforms.

As already mentioned, the earliest request for more participation and for a direct line of responsibility occurred at the local level. Through a successful popular *referendum,*[29] Parliament was "encouraged to enact law 142/1990 regulating the elections and administrative activities of the municipalities.[30] The most evident and practical result of this reform has been the direct election of mayors without the intermediary role of the political parties. The system chosen is majoritarian (winner take all) with run-off elections in case of a tie. Albeit this was the least urgent of the reforms, it is one which has proven fundamental for the development of the "revolutionary" spirit.[31]

After this experience, the negative effects of *partitocrazia* spurred the desire to limit the role of the national political parties in determining the policies and duration of the central government. A more direct democracy was seen as a possible channel for greater participation by the people and as a means to establish a "morale mandate" with parliamentarians, since the constitution does not sanction this form of control.[32] The instrument chosen to achieve these results was once again to change the electoral law. Italians decided to follow one more time the procedure sanctioned by Article 75, and they had recourse to a *referendum* in order to abrogate the proportional representation electoral law. The vote expressed[33] was so clearly in favor of abrogating the existing law that Parliament would have had no other choice than to write a new one, although the one it did approve was only a partial fulfillment of the desires of the people.[34]

The new electoral law, which was implemented for the first time in the 1994 elections, forced the parties to form coalitions before the elections in order to conquer enough support in the proportional quota and to demonstrate to the people that they were to reform multipartitism towards a two-party system. The 1996 elections helped narrow the field of contenders, and each coalition nominated a candidate to the Presidency of the Council of Ministers before the official campaign started. (**Table 2**) There has been, however, no amendment to the Constitution towards a pure parliamentary system, nor have new regulations been approved to reduce the field of political actors. The procedures to appoint the President of the Council of Ministers, as well as the requirement of a vote of confidence by both Houses, are thus still in effect. Although the President of the Republic accelerated the consultations which customarily precede the nomination, the new government, led by Prodi, did not receive the vote of confidence until a month after the election. It became apparent, then, to the majority of the people that the reform of the electoral law alone, or the recourse to the provisions of Article 75 could not introduce a coherent new form of government nor a new and more decentralized state.

Thus multipartitism, minorities and the sovereignty of the people were to be safeguarded with the institution, in January 1997, of a bicameral committee for constitutional revisions.[35] This was the third committee of the kind in a decade. The first committee was created by a joint decision of both Houses of Parliament in the mid-1980s, the second one was created by the same procedure followed for the third, in 1993, and was presided over by the honorable Nilde Jotti and Ciriaco De Mita. The procedure followed by Parliament in creating the latter two committees was by adoption of a constitutional law which was supposed to guarantee broad support for the success of the project.[36] The first two of these committees having failed to accomplish the reforms, the third one, presided by the honorable Massimo D'Alema, was given, by the law which instituted it, a timetable and a specific list of subject matters to be amended. The Committee was, in fact, to elaborate an organic revision of the entire second part of the Constitution, known as the part on the "organization of the Republic" and specifically to revise the form of state, the form of government, bicameralism and the system of guarantees.

While there was broad skepticism about the reforms in general, this was due more to a mistrust of the true reformist desires of politicians rather than to the actual accomplishments of the reforms. The expectations for success of this third bicameral committee were high, and the media and the Italian people kept a daily watch on its progress. The Committee prepared a full draft of the second part of the Constitution within the time frame the law had specified for completion of its task. A new quasi-federal Italy with a strong executive and a President of the Republic elected directly by the people, having wider powers because of its new political strength, represented but a few of the innovations introduced by the Bicameral Committee. (**Table 3**)

The elaborations of the Bicameral Committee were never presented to the nation for approval[37] and thus the most well-planned introduction of revisions to the Constitution of the last twenty years was brought to a drastic halt. The political harmony — so unusual for Italy — among the various actors in the Bicameral Committee suddenly was broken when it came time to vote the final draft of that part of the project dedicated to the judiciary and to guarantees. The negative vote represented in many ways the culmination of that other aspect of the "peaceful revolution" which had developed and progressed at the same time with the increased demands for reforms characterizing the Italian transition. That is, what the media has called "clean hands operation". This was an action by the judiciary, suddenly awakened to political and industrial corruption, which by prosecuting the elite of the political and financial cadres of the nation placed in evidence the dire need for reforms. By the time the Bicameral Committee had reached the final stages of its task, many of the court trials, which had stemmed from the "clean hands" investigation had been completed or had come to sentence. Among the reforms introduced in the draft constitution was the separation of careers between judges and prosecutors, the accountability of the justices and a drastic revision of the functions of the High Council of the judiciary. The judiciary resisted these innovations, which were perceived as diminishing their independence and autonomy. The center-left coalition tried to concede to the judiciary; the center-right coalition accused the majority of weakness. The revision of the Constitution and the labor of five intense months came to an abrupt halt.

The Committee had not been the only institution working towards the completion of the transition. Many other changes had been introduced and more were to be introduced, transforming Italy into a system of government rather different from the fundamental law of 1948 and still not yet a new coherent Republic. Among the reforms introduced by Parliament, some were accomplished by passing ordinary laws and some by constitutional laws. Some were introduced at the local and some at the national level. All, however, have contributed to the transition from the "old" towards the "new," which is yet to come.

Law 241/1990 introduced at the town council level the role of the *difensore civico*. His functions, mode of appointment and extension of his powers differ slightly from those of his equivalent in other countries, resulting, in fact, in an *ombudsman* in charge of supervising and investigating the functioning of the administrative offices, with powers to initiate disciplinary actions and make censures when citizens have been improperly denied their rights. Law 273 later integrated this law in 1995, introducing the same role at the regional level.

Another novelty introduced in the last two decades is the independent agencies. These were to follow the American model of the independent regulatory agencies, but developed along a different pattern assuming a typically Italian *genus*.[38] From a timid appearance on the institutional scene, they have now multiplied, covering almost every segment of activities.[39] A specific law creates each agency, and each agency has different tasks assigned. Furthermore, each agency determines its internal regulations and sets its agenda of priorities within a very large and elastic framework determined by Parliament in the bill creating it. All agencies are presided by officers appointed by the President of the Republic, yet each presiding officer has a different mandate and tenure in office. Still to be determined are such fundamental questions as whether these agencies are to be arbiters of the good execution of the laws or a fourth branch of the government, and whether or not there should be a law (a constitutional law perhaps) bringing uniformity to the regulations regarding their creation, performance, tenure, accountability and disciplinary powers.

Constitutional law 1/1999 brought the Regions one step closer to devolution,[40] introducing the popular election of the presiding officer and granting the latter more powers in the realm of administration. The most relevant juridical element introduced by the amendment is the normative power attributed to the Regions in as far as re-writing their statutes and choosing their own form of government. (**Table 4**) The devolution of normative power to the Regions has made the change towards a new Senate more feasible. This reform had been requested by the people[41] for the longest time and would answer two sets of problems: decentralization and a smoother and faster legislative process. The 1948 Constitution has adopted perfect bicameralism, which implied that both Houses are perfectly equal and have the same powers and competence. A highly decentralized State might, instead, look to the possibility of adopting the "imperfect" model whereupon the Senate would either be the Regional Chamber as that of the United States Senate or the German *Bundesrat,*[42] or it would be given very limited powers as Great Britain's House of Lords or Spain's *Senado*.[43]

The last in time, but certainly not the least important of the reforms introduced during this transition, has been the amendment to Article 111 of the Constitution.[44] It is one further step towards the reform of the Italian judiciary. By this amendment, in fact, the legislative branch has introduced as a Constitutional principle, fairness during a trial (**Table 5**). In fact, as of the November 1999 reform, the accused can avail himself of the right to redress the party who has made the accusation; the impartiality and the third party role of the judge have been sanctioned; a reasonable length for the trial has been affirmed, as well as an equal stand for the defense and the prosecution. The scholarly community is not unanimous in celebrating the introduction of these principles in the Constitution. There are those who affirm that the Constitution already guaranteed these rights under the general umbrella of the Bill of Rights,[45] others who thought they should be spelled out, and finally, there are those who took that the fact that Parliament felt the necessity to elaborate on Article 111 as an accusation against the judiciary.

Only a few and the most emblematic revisions have been mentioned here. These were selected in order to intricate for non-Italians the breath and length of the changes the written Constitution has undergone since the "peaceful revolution" or the "transition" has begun. By the failure of the Bicameral Committees, by the intensive recourse to the amending process, and by the stronger role of praxis, those revisions which have taken place have been accomplished piecemeal, and thus the country has lost the chance for an organic and holistic revision.

## THE PRESIDENCY

It seems therefore appropriate to make an in depth analysis of the powers the Constitution granted the President of the Republic. It is likewise appropriate to look at the procedure by which the first ten Presidents have been elected.

Since Italy is, by choice of the Constituent Assembly, a Parliamentary system, and since the Legislative branch is the only depositary of the sovereignty of the people, the constitution provides for the election of the President by Parliament in joint session integrated by three representatives[46] for each Region except for Valle d'Aosta, which is represented by one delegate only.[47]

This particular composition of the electoral college, which is integrated by regional delegates, underlines that the Head of State represents not only the State itself but the State as a community, that is to say the whole national political community. This provision aims, therefore, to include the regions — who in turn represents local autonomies — in the institutional dynamics, while widening the basis for consensus and providing for a more significant role of minorities.[48]

The President of the Chamber of Deputies (the Speaker of the House) will preside over this special assembly just as it is his or her duty to convene the assembly thirty days before the expiration of the President's tenure in office.[49] Likewise, the Speaker holds the responsibility to call for and preside over the election of the President of the Republic when he can no longer hold the office either because of death, resignation, or impeachment. Between such events and the election of a new President, the powers shall be invested in the President of the Senate who, precisely because of his potential to hold the presidential office, is excluded by all processes aimed at verifying the existence of a true impediment.

The election of the President of the Republic is by secret ballot.[50] The secrecy of the vote is important, because it is aimed at guaranteeing that the President truly represent the community as a whole without political ties.[51] Unlike the original provisions in the American Constitution for the election of the President of the United States of America,[52] the Italian Constitution does not foresee the possibility of two candidates balloting for the President's office.[53] In fact the Constitution provides for the President to be elected with the majority of two-thirds of the assembly. This very high *quorum* stands for the first three ballots and aims at guaranteeing the widest possible majority within both Houses integrated by the delegates: the national political community. The very high *quorum* was also introduced as a "check" or a guarantee against the possibility of a party or a coalition representing few parties taking over and manipulating the office of the President.[54] The election methodology, which was adopted by the Italian Constitution, is once again a compromise between two opposite ideas. In the Constituent Assembly, in fact, some wished to have the direct election of the President by the people, while others wished to limit participation in the vote only to the members of Parliament. It is thus that the enlargement, albeit minimal, of the Electoral College through the integration of the representatives of the Regional Councils, was sanctioned. This again was in order to underline and to guarantee the role the new Head of State was supposed to hold.

The last, yet certainly not the least important provision dealing with the procedure for electing the President is the one foreseeing the eventuality of requiring many ballots. Thus the Constitution sanctions that "*after the third ballot an absolute majority is sufficient.*"[55]

With the exception of three cases, since 1946 all Presidents have been elected after the third ballot, and, with the exception of the tenth President, Carlo Azeglio Ciampi, all have been elected under the proportional electoral law. Furthermore, as yet another anomaly of the Italian parliamentary system, the candidate to the highest institutional appointment was also decided by the *conventio ad excludendum*, a *criterium* by which, if the opposition (leftist parties) was to be excluded from the government, it was to be assigned the chairmanship of either House[56] while alternating the Presidency between a Christian Democrat and a non-Christian Democrat.[57] It soon became apparent to those who followed Italian politics, that the more one party tried to break the alternation pattern or to "occupy" an additional seat, the longer the time span before the successful election and the higher the number of ballots required. (**Table 6**).

The only occasions in recent years in which a President was elected on the first ballot, were Francesco Cossiga in 1985[58] and Carlo Azeglio Ciampi in 1999.[59] Both times there was an "open" ante-election consultation on the qualities required in order to become President at that specific juncture in time.

The majority of citizens could meet the requirements necessary to be elected,[60] although the position is totally incompatible with any other employment.[61] A stipend and official facilities for the performance of his duties are provided for by the State.[62] Thus, even the poorest of citizens is theoretically eligible.

Throughout the last fifty years Parliament sought the President from among its own. Only Ciampi can be considered extraneous to the political cadres, a non-professional politician, although he had been Prime Minister[63] and Minister of the Treasury.[64]

The requirement that the President be at least fifty years old is aimed to guarantee that the highest appointment in the country falls upon a person who has reached maturity, experience, and the necessary authority in order to execute such an important and delicate task. Although the Constitution is silent on the subject, it has become constitutional convention that the President of the Republic, as soon as the election is over, resigns from all previously held appointments in a political party. It is fitting that the President, the Head of State, and the representative of the political community at large, should be free and independent of any political faction.

It is, indeed, the overwhelming desire to assure the independence of the President of the Republic, which, in the end, inspired the Constituent Assembly to provide him with an extended tenure in office.[65] This tenure is longer than that of the legislature which elected him; hence he should not feel committed to it,[66] thereby underlining his impartiality. A second factor, which influenced the decision of the Italian Founding Fathers, was the idea that it would require time to acquire the necessary expertise in the office. Last, but certainly not least relevant, the seven years tenure underlines further the role the President ought to have in the mediation among the various political parties specifically after an electoral consultation in which the forces within Parliament have shifted.[67] The Constitution does not regulate, nor does it veto a second mandate, yet no President has expressed the desire to be elected for a second term.[68] The possibility of a second mandate leads one to believe that the Constituent Assembly timidly introduced political responsibility for the President of the Republic, as it had done for the Government.[69]

## THE POWERS OF THE PRESIDENT

Presidential powers are clearly enumerated in the constitution and, unlike its counterpart in the United States, in order to prevent authoritative "surprises," no power can be implied. Albeit enumerated, the powers are not always well-defined, thus, giving each President of the Republic the possibility to interpret the powers as befitting the occasion. Several classifications of the presidential powers can, however, be made.

The first distinction that can be made is according to the functions of the State. We can thus distinguish between acts that relate to the legislative,[70] executive[71] and judicial spheres.[72] (**Tables 7,8,9**).

The functional *criterium* allows us to distinguish presidential powers according to the proclaimed goal. We may have, then, acts aimed at controlling,[73] participating, blocking,[74] stimulating, etc.

A third *criterium* distinguishes the powers on the participation, or lack thereof, of other institutional actors. There are powers that are solely — in form and substance — presidential;[75] others that are presidential in form but need the assumption of responsibility by the executive;[76] and others yet that are substantially of the executive, yet require the approval of the President of the Republic.[77] The assumption of responsibility by the ministers is formalized by the *controfirma*[78] and the approval by the President of the Republic, by authorizing the presentation of governmental draft laws to the Houses.

Before analyzing, albeit briefly, the powers as enumerated in the Constitution,[79] it seems appropriate to explain the significance of two fundamental presidential tools which represent the continuity with the constitutional monarchy while being innovative in a parliamentary system. In order to appreciate fully the depth of the powers sanctioned by the constitution of 1948 for the President of the Republic, it is necessary to understand the exact meaning of the presidential authorization for governmental draft bills and the *controfirma*, both of which represent, in fact, a link with the past.

The authorization to introduce to Parliament bills initiated by the government is a residual power from the days of the monarchy when the king, the Head of State, was also the Head of the Government, and it was he who authorized his own ministers to take the legislative initiative. Presently it is not easy to classify this power, especially since it is usually employed in conjunction with the power of the Head of State to promulgate those laws which have been already approved by Parliament. It certainly should be considered a check upon the legitimacy and the constitutional opportunity of bills designed by the government.

The *controfirma* is yet another residue from the monarchical regime, during which time the instrument was used to exonerate the king from all responsibility. Without it in the past no act by the king was considered legitimate. In the Republican Constitution it has a different relevance, since the President of the Republic may not and should not be considered totally without political responsibility for the actions he does undertake, since he is subject to criticism like everybody else. It is not necessary to have the *controfirma* for those acts in which the President participates but for which he is not responsible.[80]

*a). Head of State.* The President is the highest officer of the State. He is free from traditional powers and cannot be in any way considered part of the government or of the public administration, although the constitution[81] empowers him with functions which can be considered either governmental and/or administrative.

*b). The power to send messages.* This is typically solely a presidential power. In this case the president in fact expresses his own opinion in a written form as a control (check) on the legislative branch or to propose a new legislative course or yet to denounce possible violations of the constitution.[82]

*c). The power to call the elections.* (Art. 87.3) The life of a legislature has been determined to be of five years. The Constituent Assembly had opted for a "perfect" bicameral system in which both Chambers were to hold the same powers while representing different constituencies and being composed of men and women of diverse age segments of the community. The only "unequal" element between the Houses was to be the length of the legislature. Yet in 1963, an amendment was approved establishing a five year life expectancy for both. Whether because the natural deadline has been reached or because the President has exercised his power to dissolve the Houses, it is a presidential prerogative officially to set the date for and call the election to renew Parliament.

*d). The power to authorize presentation of governmental draft bills to the Houses.* This is yet another power the President of the Republic inherited from those of the King who was the chief executive and therefore had to approve of all draft bills before they were introduced to the legislative branch for discussion and approval. Albeit scholars are not in agreement[83] in classifying this power, the same should be considered a check on the executive.

*e). The power to promulgate the laws.* (Art.73.1) Unlike the previous regime, the President does not participate in the legislative process and thus, unlike the King, his role is purely formal. The promulgation falls, in fact, in the last steps of the lawmaking process when the legislative branch has completed the law. It may not be considered part of the legislative process; rather it is more appropriate to consider it a check performed by the "neuter" President to ascertain a) that both the Houses have, indeed, voted upon the exact same text, and b) that the new law is indeed pursuant to the constitution.[84] The exercise of this power is one of those cases in which some scholars saw the President of the Republic as "notary" of actions initiated by others, rather than as an actor himself.[85]

*f). The power to call a referendum.* Referenda are the only real instrument of direct democracy left to citizens of contemporary democracies. The Constituent Assembly did not deem it safe for the democratic regime, which had just been established in Italy, to sanction the possibility for the people to propose a *referendum* so that only the abrogative form was contemplated: "*A popular referendum shall be held to abrogate, totally or partially, a law . . . when requested by five hundred thousand electors.*"[86]

When the people have requested it, and the Central Office of the Court of Cassation has controlled the lawful fulfillment of all provisions, and the Constitutional Court has declared the question legitimate and not falling within the sphere of the laws, articles and provisions which are not to be amended,[87] then and only then can the President of the Republic call the *referendum*. The difficulty of the process in order to hold such a vote and the variety of organs involved clearly denote that it was an instrument to be used exceptionally and not as a political tool, as it has been in the 1990s.

g). *The power to nominate*. This is yet another power which could be easily identified as a remnant of the monarchy. It has, in time, been re-defined several times, the latest being in 1991, half way into this long transition which Italy has been experiencing. Each of these interventions has made possible the actual elaboration of categories of nominations which can be traced back to two larger families: a) the nominations which can fully be considered solely presidential; and b) the nominations which are governmental in nature yet presidential in form, requiring that the President of the Republic countersign the act of nomination.

While all belong to the general family of nominations, we must distinguish further those nominations which can be considered acted upon because of a specific presidential platform or agenda[88] from those which fall mainly among those acts necessary in order for the state to work.[89] The former nominations can thus be defined as being of political nature, while the latter belong unquestionably to the administrative realm.

*h). The diplomatic power*. The diplomatic power encompasses both the representation abroad[90] and the domestic duties of accreditation of foreign dignitaries, as well as the ratification of the treaties after the Houses have converted them into law. Most controversial among the diplomatic sphere are the war powers since the Constitution bestows upon the President of the Republic the power to declare war, after a decision in favor of it by both Houses.[91] While the latter must not be a law, a legislative act is necessary in order to empower the executive with the "necessary powers". It is after having taken all these steps that the President of the Republic can exercise the power to declare war. It should be further noted that, according to the constitution, Italy recognizes only one kind of war and that is a defensive war.[92]

It must be assumed then that these provisions were devised by the Constituent Assembly in order to underline the centrality of the legislative branch, which cannot be superseded not even in times of war.[93]

i). *Commander of the armed forces*. Like its counterpart in the United States of America the President of the Italian Republic is commander in-chief of the armed forces. And, as with the former, also the latter was granted this role by the constitution in order to ensure the supremacy of civilians over the military.[94]

j). *President of the Supreme Council for Defense*. As the Commander of the armed forces, the President of the Republic is also the presiding officer of the Supreme Defense Council. This Council is composed of eight permanent members: the President of the Republic, the President of the Council of Ministers, five ministers (foreign affairs, interior, treasury, defense, and industry) and the Joint Chief of Staff (*Capo di Stato Maggiore della Difesa*). At times of peace, the latter is directly responsible to the Minister of Defense, thus again underlining the absence of political responsibility for the military, as well as for the President of the Republic.

k). *President of the High Council of the Judiciary*. This is the only case in which the President of the Republic enters into relations with the judiciary as an independent order. In fact the nomination of one third of the judges of the Supreme Court falls into another category, the Court being a constitutional organ above and separated from the judiciary. This is not just a formal power of the President, since he presides over the High Council and sets its agenda. There are several theories about why the Constituent Assembly chose to include the President in the activities of the Council.[95] Some commentators argue that since the President is the presiding officer of the Council, the latter is a constitutionally recognized branch of government equivalent to the legislative and the executive.[96] A larger number of commentators argue that the Council is merely an administrative office and that the presence of the Head of State as the presiding officer can be interpreted as a mechanism for protecting participatory democracy, because the President represents and guarantees national unity.[97]

The President of the Republic presides, as noted previously, when the Council sits as a whole. In all other cases the High Council is presided by its Vice President who serves as chair in the President's absence and when the disciplinary sections is convened. The limits of the Vice President's powers in relation to the President's became an issue during the presidential term of Francesco Cossiga (1985-92). He was often engaged in public conflict with the High Council, and the Constitutional Court was finally called upon to resolve the controversy over the attribution of powers. The Court's conclusion was that the Vice President is allowed to act in the absence of the President, but this does not imply any honorary attribution of powers.[98]

*l). The power to grant pardons and commute punishments.* This is perhaps the strongest and most clear remnant of the monarchical privileges. The text is identical to the provision of Article 8 of the Albertine Statute.[99] Until 1992[100] it included also the provision to grant an amnesty.[101] In fact, the intention of the Constituent Assembly was that this provision be interpreted along with Article 79 which used to attribute the power to grant amnesties and pardons to the President of the Republic on the basis of a law of delegation of the Houses.

*m). The power to confer honors.* By this power the President of the Republic can bestow honors upon individuals or institutions that have distinguished themselves in particular activities. The President may not create new honors but can only bestow the honors within the five existing categories which have been established by law. To those who have distinguished themselves in the sciences, letters, arts, economics and public offices the President may bestow the Order of Merit of the Italian Republic. To no more than twenty-five men and women who have distinguished themselves in the field of work, the President may confer the Order of Merit for Work. The Military Order of Italy may be bestowed upon servicemen who have accomplished heroic actions while at war. The Order of the Italian Star is bestowed upon Italian citizens who reside abroad. Lastly, to servicemen who distinguished themselves during World War I or previous wars the

President was free to bestow the Order of Vittorio Veneto.

*n). The power to dissolve Parliament.* This is perhaps one of the most powerful weapons the Constitution attributes to the President of the Republic. He must hear the opinion of the Presidents of both Houses, but their opinion is not binding, and final responsibility for the decision is solely his.[102] The only other limitation on the recourse to dissolving Parliament clearly sanctioned in the Constitution is a prohibition to recur to such a drastic solution during the last six months of his mandate unless this period coincides with the last six months of the legislature.[103]

The extent to which the use of this power can become a means to introduce and affirm a political platform or agenda will be discussed later,[104] it is sufficient here to clarify the intentions of the Constituent Assembly. The fear of a strong President inspired the assemblymen to move political power away from the new Head of State. Yet if the country was to be in danger of or at a halt because of Parliament's incapacity to overcome political squabbling, or if the executive were to lose the confidence of its majority in both Houses, and this majority could not be recomposed, then the President of the Republic should be enabled to dissolve the Houses and call for a new election which would define presumably a new and clear majority.

The limit on the last six months of the presidential mandate was introduced in order to prevent an attempt by the President to obtain a more favorable House for his possible re-election.[105]

*o). The power to dissolve town, provincial and regional councils.* The transition has perhaps affected mostly the regional organization and the relation the regions have with the State.[106] The 1948 Constitution had devised a unique decentralization pattern called regionalism which, in the intention of the assemblymen, was supposed to be half way between the federal and the decentralized model. Territorial entities such as towns, provinces and regions were to enjoy high levels of political, normative, statutory, administrative and financial autonomy. This was perhaps the less fulfilled part of the Constitution.

The councils of the regional governments became elective in the mid 1970s and the reform of these territorial units is still underway. A clear enumeration of their powers can be found in the original version of the 1948 Constitution;[107] recent amendments[108] have drastically increased those powers turning the Regions into stronger territorial entities and devolving more power to their executives.[109] Notwithstanding these drastic changes, the President of the Republic can still dissolve each of the territorial councils when these have passed acts contrary to the Constitution or have performed grave violations of the law. The dissolution can also occur for reasons of national security.[110]

*p). The power to nominate the President of the Council of Ministers.* This is yet another power in which the President of the Republic should be free and sole in making the appointment, although it is yet another act for which the counter signature is required.[111] Scholars are in agreement that in reality the President is not really free to appoint the President of the Council of Ministers since he must take into consideration the political orientation of the electorate as reflected in the composition of Parliament.[112]

Albeit the Constitution is silent on the criteria for selecting the President of the Council of Ministers, a few rules can be drawn from constitutional conventions:

1) The President of the Republic may not appoint a President of the Council who will certainly lack the confidence of the Houses in order to dissolve them.[113]

2) The President of the Republic, in order to maintain its "neutrality," should avoid helping the appointee in drafting the agenda of the future Council.[114]

3) The President of the Republic may overcome a refusal to countersign the act of dissolution of the Houses by appointing a new government just for ordinary administration and for running of election.[115]

*q). The power to convene Parliament in extraordinary session.* It is a *stimulus* power since the President of the Republic could wish to solicit Parliament to act whenever its inaction could damage or threaten the constitutional order. The Constitution mandates that both Houses shall be convened, thus respecting perfect bicameralism.[116] Since 1948 this power has never been exercised.

*r). The power to nominate judges on the Constitutional Court.* This is undoubtedly and most obviously one of the solely presidential powers. The President, in fact, can appoint one third of the Court, choosing among judges, full university professors and lawyers with at least twenty years practice.[117] Just as his counterpart in the United States, the President of the Republic should not be influenced by political partisanship[118] in appointing the judges on the Constitutional Court for a non-renewable nine years' mandate.

*s). The power to nominate life senators.* This is yet again clearly a presidential power since it implies going beyond political constraints. The presidential character of this power is emphasized by the mere enumeration of the qualities future appointees should meet in order to become life senators.[119]

This is intended to be a solely presidential power, since the nomination of life senators can alter the *equilibrium* among the political parties. The only controversy over this clearly stated power, was generated during the mandate of President Cossiga when he raised the question whether each President could nominate five life Senators or if only five at a time could be in office.[120]

*t). The power to request a second deliberation of a bill.* The President of the Republic may request of the Houses a second deliberation before promulgating a law by accompanying the bill with a message explaining the perplexities and the motives of the request. The President can only request this second deliberation when the law appears to be in contrast with the Constitution or when the President of the Republic perceives it to be in disparity with the general interests of the national community of which, as the Head of State, he is guarantor. This power cannot be compared to the veto power of the President of the United States of America since it does not require an overriding of the presidential request. It encompasses only a new debate, not a new drafting of the law.[121]

## THE PRESIDENCY IN TRANSITION

The purpose of this section of the lecture is to analyze the role and functions of the President of the Republic throughout the last fifteen years, to place in evidence how these have shifted away from the normative path, and to attempt to evaluate if, indeed, a constitutional praxis has settled in.

There is no doubt, in fact, that the role of the Head of

State, representative of national unity and guarantor of the respect of the constitutional order, has been slowly moving from a role of arbiter to one of actor upon the political scene. The hypothesis is that the transitional period, which Italy has been undergoing, has affected the Presidency more than any other constitutional order because of the flexibility of the former, favoring the establishing of a new role and functions for the President of the Republic. This in turn will hardly be discarded whenever the political actors will decide to adapt the written constitution to the material one. At the same time, the new role and functions of the President of the Republic can be seen as elements characterizing a new regime, in many and important ways quite different from the one envisioned in 1948.

The President of the Republic, while still maintaining the attributions of guarantor, might be using the powers of stimulus not to defend the constitutional order, but rather to push forward the completion of the transition. It is necessary, therefore, to be able to determine whether the political program, initiated by the Head of State is "an integrating function of a supreme goal and thus . . . activates a change in the constitution" or whether the same political program is that of a political group which has prevailed over the others instituting a diverse order.[122] In order to determine this, an attempt will be made to avoid giving too much emphasis to concrete cases, although these are necessary to determine a new constitutional praxis. In fact, "If too much emphasis were to be given to the material constitution, it would be fatal to evaluate the system subjectively and unilaterally. The conclusions would inevitably be different, with regard both to the particular and to the general problem. Lacking the normative element to which it is appropriate to anchor the investigation, it would be easy, however, to fall unconsciously into sociology. It is appropriate, instead, to evaluate the concrete behavior of the various institutions and the praxis which was instituted by the behavior of certain groups or organs, either to avoid constitutional mandates or to impose the respect for the system in the terms imposed by the Constitution."[123]

In order to evaluate the existence of a praxis it will be necessary to evaluate the interpretation of the exact nature of the powers, briefly described earlier, which were given by the Presidents of the Republic. Italy being a civil law country, the analysis of the praxis will have to be only in connection with the actual norm in order to measure how far away from this it has actually strayed.[124]

It seems appropriate, at this point, to look back at the functions with which the Constituent Assembly empowered the President of the Republic in the application of the role he was to hold as guarantor of the stability of the regime.

Unquestionable that the spirit which animated the assemblymen was one of rejection of an authoritarian regime. They were troubled,[125] in fact, almost constantly by the concern to recognize and eliminate all those institutional mechanisms which had either favored the establishment of the authoritarian regime or had helped it negate those participatory freedoms which, from the *Risorgimento* onward, had represented the *leit-motif* of the pendulum of empowerment between the Crown and Parliament.[126] It is this conflict, which gave birth to the first and second representative regimes. The latter was dramatically interrupted by the advent of the fascist regime in 1922, before it could have reached the new equilibrium sought with the introduction of new political forces through the electoral reform of 1913.[127] The *coup* inevitably broke the constitutional continuity, generating a new unbalanced relationship between the executive and the legislative branches which would mature during the Resistance and the Transitory regime, when it would be the Committee for National Liberation which would assume the executive powers.[128]

After June 2, 1946, in view of the results of the institutional referendum,[129] it was the Constituent Assembly which resolved the balance between the executive and the legislative in determining the exact nature of the relationship between the Government (the executive) and Parliament, on the one hand, and the Head of State, on the other hand. The Head of State was expected to hold a "guarantee" function and was invested with the role of representative of the national unity instead of representing the nation.

The new Head of State replaced almost "automatically" the King in all those functions which had developed throughout the Statutory, Fascist and Transitional regimes.[130] Contrary to the King in the statutory regime,[131] the President of the Republic was to represent the national unity, that is to say he was to represent the permanent existence of the State, above all changes.

The President of the Republic, must therefore hold a neutral role among the political forces; he must protect the Constitution because of his role as guarantor, and he is expected to ensure the respect for the laws and for constitutional values;[132] he is invested with a sort of "influential magistrature", by which he is expected to counsel, to reprimand and to encourage the government.[133] Thus, the assemblymen sanctioned within the positive law the role of check, break, initiative and balance of the President of the Republic.

Scholars are in agreement on the fact that the Constitution formally does not invest the President of the Republic with the function of forming the political agenda. At the same time scholars cannot deny the fact that the powers of the President can affect and do affect the political platform of the Government.[134]

In the execution of his powers, the President does exercise, indeed, an influence on the determination of the political platform, while he ascertains the correct execution of the constitutional functions of the other branches by resorting to the powers of impulse, restraint and check.

Of all the powers already mentioned, albeit briefly,[135] there are a few which seem appropriate to the analysis at hand. In fact, the power to send messages to Parliament, the power to nominate the President of the Council of Ministers and the power to dissolve the Houses can undoubtedly be considered powers of stimulus and thus can be used as variables in an attempt to measure the shift from a neutral to an active role of the Italian President of the Republic.[136]

### *The Power of Message*

The constituent assemblymen specifically sanctioned the power to send messages, while defining its form and limits.[137] As a rule all messages must be countersigned[138] in order to give them validity and to establish the responsibility of the government for its content.

A restrictive reading of the power to send messages may lead to limiting President's ability to use this. In fact, according to this school of thought, as the representative of national unity the

President of the Republic should use this power, always with the countersignature and only on occasion of speeches held while abroad, to the armed forces, to the High Council of the Judiciary and in press communications. Following this restrictive reading of the Constitution "any use of this a typical manifestation of thought which might have political innuendos should be avoided."[139]

Nevertheless, there should be no further doubt that presidential messages, because they are addressed to the representatives of popular sovereignty, are indeed presidential acts which set a political trend for which the countersignature should have merely a formal value[140] or, at the most, be a check on the constitutional correctness of the message itself. The only message which does not require the countersignature is the message delivered to the Houses in joint session integrated by the regional delegates, on the occasion of the swearing in of the new President.[141]

It was during the presidency of Francesco Cossiga (1985-1992) that a new and diverse interpretation of the form and limitation of the power of messages could be noticed.[142] Although some significant symptoms can be found already in the preceding seven year term. On the occasion of the fortieth anniversary of the Republic, President Cossiga read a commemorative message to the Houses. It must be said that the majority of the scholarly community is oriented to interpret this first "unusual" message to the Houses as a "message/speech".[143] Furthermore, it is during this same mandate, that the President of the Republic sent another "unusual" message to the Houses. This was neither the swearing-in message, nor a message inviting the Houses to reconsider a law, nor a commemorative message, but a stimulus message.[144] The fact that the message was not only received by Parliament, but also followed by a debate investigating possible solutions and time tables to act upon the requests of the President is indicative of a new praxis settling in.

The positive reaction given by the Houses to the message sent by Cossiga encouraged his successors to use this instrument more freely and more frequently both as a tool for stimulating the other branches and as a means to affirm a presidential platform. Thus, in his message to the Houses after the swearing-in, President Ciampi enumerated the reforms, which he believed necessary to "lead our political system towards European constitutional modernity".[145]

Having proposed his program, the Head of State elaborated on it in detailed messages, addresses and interventions. From all of the above, it can easily be concluded that the President of the Republic has interpreted his role as guarantor of the Constitution in an active key, pursuing it through urging the completion of the reforms process. It is true that the message to the High Council of the Judiciary encompasses the same arguments introduced in his message to the Houses for the swearing-in, yet, in the former, there are traces of more in-depth analysis and a clearer, more detailed platform. The President even recommends the means to reach the affirmed goals.

### *The "Power" to Manifest*

Contrary to the power of message, the power to manifest one's thoughts or to deliver an oral message is not enumerated in the Constitution and is regulated by conventional rules.[146] From the early days, however, the Presidents of the Republic have considered it a power, which, not requiring the countersignature, is more effective and more opportune for the fulfillment of the constitutional role of stimulus. The recourse to it by President Gronchi, especially while on his trips abroad, elevates this instrument to a true exercise of power,[147] albeit it is appropriate to repeat that, formally, the only way to explain the power to manifest is the symptomatic and episodic epiphany of the crisis of the constitutional order.[148]

The recourse to the power to manifest, subjected to prior communication to the Government, was at first occasional, but reached relevant levels during the mandate of President Pertini. It could be said, in fact, that it was the recourse by that President to the so-called free manifestation which offers the best evidence of the political significance of this instrument.[149]

During the last two years of the mandate of President Cossiga, the recourse to the power to manifest reached more incisive levels, yet it is with the mandate of president Scalfaro that it reaches the frequency and tenor of "intrusiveness" in the spheres of the Government and of Parliament, even in open disagreement with the political platform of the former.[150]

Progressively, therefore, the President of the Republic have made recourse to the "power to manifest" to set in motion both the transition in general and the transition of the presidential powers. The significance of "the power to manifest" should not be underestimated, in fact, in the evolution of the functions and role of the President of the Republic as the representative of the national unity and hence of all the Italian people.[151] It is this transition from an office "remote" to the everyday necessities of the people to one which represents and gives voice to them, which has allowed the change in role and the increased the functions of the Head of State, even though he is not titular of any representation.[152]

The reach of the power to manifest is transformed, thus, from a means to stimulate debates and policies into a power to check upon the inaction of the other branches. The increase in manifestations of thought has also affected the other presidential powers, even those which could more easily be considered powers of stimulus. It should be repeated, however, that the Constitution of 1948 did not attribute such power to the President of the Republic. This is because the executive power and the related power of setting the political agenda falls upon the Government, which is the only power to hold a "fiduciary relation" with parliament, and which, in turn, is the only institution representing the sovereignty of the people.

### *The Power to Nominate the President of the Council of Ministers*

Among those powers more commonly considered as "programming," it is unquestionably appropriate to include the power to nominate the President of the Council of Ministers.[153] Scholars unanimously agree in considering this a solely presidential power, since the minister countersigning the nomination is a consenting actor.[154] However, scholars are also fully in agreement in affirming the limited discretion the President of the Republic can exercise, since he must take into consideration the political orientation of the people as expressed in the elections. His perception of the latter and his consequential decision will have to be, in turn, followed by and, in a way, approved by the successful vote of confidence by both Houses.[155] Without the confidence of

Parliament, the power to nominate and the discretion of the President of the Republic are null.[156]

As a rule, governments have been the expression of the political parties and have been formed by coalitions of parties. Few Presidents of the Republic[157] have made recourse to a "holistic reading" of the powers enumerated in the Constitution. This has always occurred at times of crisis of the political equilibrium or of transformation of the system.[158] The norm in appointing the Presidents of the Council of Ministers has been according to the reading of Articles 92-94. Yet the fact that on occasions the President of the Republic has deemed it necessary, useful or practical to alter the norm, and that these occasions have always been in cases of crisis or of transformation, and that the most recent Heads of State have deemed i t necessary to appoint "technical governments" prove that Italy is undergoing yet another transformation.

The term in office of President Scalfaro has been particularly important for the evolution of this power. The majority of the nominations of Presidents of the Council of Ministers made by him have been, in fact, in open contradiction with the criteria analyzed, albeit briefly, earlier.[159] That is to say that President Scalfaro did not approach a government crisis or the appointing of the President of the Council of Ministers according to the Constitution.

To confirm this thesis it will be sufficient to mention two cases in point. The first case was the appointment of Carlo Azeglio Ciampi, then Governor General of the Bank of Italy, who formed a government strongly composed of "technicians"[160] with a very limited agenda and deliberated with the President of the Republic. The proclaimed task of that executive was, in fact, the drafting of the electoral law before the election of the new parliament was to take place.[161]

The second case occurred when the Head of State appointed Dini to lead a so-called "technical" government.[162] This took place when the majority expressed in the elections of 1994 broke down because of the withdrawal of one of its members. Once the agenda was completed, Dini did not try to prolong his mandate and resigned.[163]

The instrumental recourse to the power to nominate the President of the Council of Ministers by Scalfaro is indicative of a presidential initiative of which a timid trace can be found in 1987 when President Cossiga nominated Fanfani in order to exercise the power to dissolve the Houses.[164]

It is not, however, and it cannot be for as long as the Constitution remains unamended, a government of the President of the Republic. In fact, the executive depends on the vote of confidence by the Houses and is responsible to them for its acts or inaction.[165]

### *The Power to Dissolve the Houses*

Last but certainly not least relevant to the subject matter at hand is the power to dissolve the Houses.[166] This power can better be defined, and has been correctly defined, as the needle of the scale keeping in equilibrium the relationship between organs.[167]

The scholarly community distinguishes several types of dissolution, based on whether it is judged in its formal pattern or for its timing. The latter category will be analyzed here. It is said to be "subsequent" dissolution when the President of the Republic has recourse to it because of a contrast between Parliament and the Government or after a vote of no confidence. It is said to be "preventive" when it is subsequent to a government crisis, which the political parties believe can only be resolved by a new election.[168]

There is a third event, believed by some scholars to justify the dissolution of Parliament by the President of the Republic, and that is when the President believes there is a definitive rupture between the nation and Parliament. This typology befits the dissolution in 1994. The President of the Republic, in fact, decided for the dissolution because he believed it inappropriate to bring the legislature to its natural term, which had begun in 1992 once the new electoral law had been approved.[169]

The founding fathers of republican Italy did not waste words or ink in defining the procedures to activate the recourse to dissolution. The President of the Republic can dissolve the Houses provided he has heard the opinion of the presiding officers. The opinion of the latter is mandatory, yet not binding. Although this is the only procedural obligation, it is the one which sheds light on the intentions of the assemblymen. It is exactly the President's duty to evaluate and to verify whether there is a possible majority in Parliament, notwithstanding the squabbling between the political parties. (**Table 10**)

Although the dissolution is an instrument defined only marginally in the Constitution, it has been the norm, since 1948, for the Presidents to resort to it only when and if they were in the presence of an otherwise unsolvable crisis. (**Table 11**) The decision whether or not to dissolve both or either House[170] is, however, unmistakably presidential,[171] as President Scalfaro reminded the nation. During his seven-year term, President Scalfaro dissolved Parliament twice,[172] denied the dissolution asked by the political parties on three occasions[173] and threatened to dissolve the Houses once.[174] While in the first dissolution of Parliament by Scalfaro, as pointed out earlier, the probable fracture between the nation and Parliament can justify the decision by the President of the Republic, it must be said that not only did the executive at the time not lose the confidence of the Houses[175] but even the President refused to accept the resignations of the former.[176] In the second dissolution, President Scalfaro decided to act only when he perceived the fulfillment of the agenda by the Executive, thus giving the birth and the death sentence to the executive he had wanted to create.

It seems evident therefore that President Scalfaro interpreted this power to be solely presidential. And it is similarly clear that the power to dissolve the Houses (or even the threat to dissolve)[177] has, indeed, become a legislative/political instrument. This turns the President of a Parliamentary Republic more presidential then the Constituent Assembly had envisioned.

## DEVELOPMENTS

The presidential praxis developed from the tenure of Einaudi to that of Scalfaro, albeit here only briefly illustrated, shows a growth of those presidential powers which direct politics and establish policies. It is the accession of this typically governmental power to the President of the Republic which illustrates more than any other power the depth of the constitutional transition the country has been experiencing. The evidence thus far gathered indicates that the transitional period is longer than what most scholars have believed. In fact, the beginning of the transition is commonly dated at 1993. This focuses upon the revision of the electoral law from proportional to quasi-majoritarian and the changes the new electoral law necessarily introduced in the relationship between the legislative and the executive branches.[178] It seems more appropriate, however, to date the transition from the presidential mandate of Cossiga as regards as the powers of stimulus and as far back as the presidential term of Pertini for the power to manifest one's platform.

The fact that the President of the Republic has acquired powers in the field of setting-up the political platform is in itself a sign that the system is experiencing malfunctions. In fact, each time the functional character of the system is obstructed, the President of the Republic becomes an active subject.[179] The exercise of presidential powers should have its limits in order to avoid a violation of the Constitution (and not to fulfill one) or the persistence of a political conflict.[180]

It is the flexible interpretation of "that enigmatic accumulation of non-homogeneous powers,"[181] and the elusiveness which hampers an organic picture of the role of the Head of State and his closeness with the highest administration, the judiciary and the executive which are significant here. They lead one to believe that the role has been modified, past, perhaps, the expectations of the other constitutional organs, although they have silently accepted the change. If, indeed, presidential powers have evolved, this has been made possible by the silent acceptance of the other organs whose hampering action could impede the epiphany and/or the rooting of these powers.

There are doubts regarding the existence of a "transition", in the common definition of the term, because a transition should be done in a much shorter period of time than the fifteen and more years of the evolution of the presidential powers. Furthermore, and again because of its duration in time, it does not seem appropriate to define this period as a "transitory regime" which would require a clear date of inception or an initiating event[182] and a clearer date of termination.[183] The "stewardship" theory does not seem befitting the Italian situation either, since in this case the Head of State is expected to lead the ship of State during a storm by concentrating all powers in his hands without checks and balances until the storm is over. The "stewardship" theory in a democratic regime requires brief time spells.

## CONCLUSIONS

Throughout the last decade the Italian people seem to have experienced a sudden awakening of previously dormant democratic and moralistic sentiments, while discovering an interest in efficiency and parliamentary productivity. The effect provoked by this apparently abrupt stirring has been called by the international media the "peaceful revolution" of Italy. Yet it may not be considered a tranquil period for the nation, just as the "crises" of the past were not at all turbulent.

While these years have not been serene, they have been characterized by non-violent protests against the system, which have undoubtedly influenced the media in their description of events. The "revolution" of Italy is physiological rather then pathological. After fifty years of participatory democracy, of schooling and higher education, of exposition by the media and other instruments of information, a majority, albeit small, of Italians, older and younger from the north as well as from the south, have physiologically come to learn and appreciate the potentialities of the fundamental law. At the same time, they have ceased to ignore the deficiencies and the pathological evolution of some institution. Hence, the calls for changes, and the "transition".

The silent conformity of the system, in the progressive establishment of a different constitutional system, even in the presence of non-written sources, is not a characteristic of a "transitory regime" nor of a Civil Law country. Having excluded the possibility of being in a transition or in a transitory regime, having further refused the applicability of the "stewardship" theory, it seems more befitting the Italian case to say that we are, indeed, in the presence of a change. This is slowly and unconsciously moving the nation away from the rigid enumeration and separation of powers so typical of Civil Law countries, and approaching to the Common Law countries. There, even though in the presence of a clear separation of powers, there are more possibilities of two branches overstepping in the same areas. The elasticity of interpretation allows for a pendulum-like alternation of forces accepted even by the highest courts as a natural and physiological contribution to the making of a mature democracy.

If all of the above is correct, the "transformation" cannot

but be slow and lasting in time, so as to allow not one organ but all organs to conform to the new. The introduction of constitutional amendments, such as the one on the fairness of trials, and of ordinary laws to assure constitutional balance among the branches, such as the electoral law, may be seen as further transformations of the original system of government. Or they may be a newly found balance between the President of the Republic and Parliament in a system in which the President has acquired political powers and must now be considered an active and vital member of the executive branch.

The fact that, during these first months of the mandate of President Ciampi, there has been a return to Article 138 of the Constitution[184] may be seen, in the opinion of this lecturer, not as the President of the Republic being remissive or trying to "guarantee" the 1948 constitutional order, but rather as the "return" of the pendulum in favor of Parliament, as typical of a common law system.[185]

We could be in the presence of yet another element in favor of the theory of "cross fertilization" which has revealed a convergence (neither intentional nor conscious) of the two main juridical families.[186]

On the other hand, the transformation has strongly reduced the rigidity of the system, allowing it to adapt to the new European Common Law. Conversely, the latter becomes stronger because of the jurisprudence of the European Court of Justice and on the capacity of each member nation to accommodate European jurisprudence in their "sovereign" states.

This, in fact, is the focal point. Are the member states still truly sovereign? Are we going to look at sovereignty through the classic dichotomy of internal and external sovereignty which prevailed until a few decades ago. This affirms sovereignty to be an essential and constituent element of the State and indicates that the superior power *superiorem non recognoscens*? [187] Or, are we going to accept sovereignty conditioned by international and communitarian relations?[188]

Having accepted the principle that a sovereign State may voluntarily relinquish a part or more parts of its original sovereignty without renouncing statehood sovereignty, it becomes easier to appreciate how the German Lander and the States in the United

States of America still consider themselves sovereign States while having ceded their external (for military defense) and economic sovereignty (in order to facilitate commerce and the execution of the principle of solidarity).[189]

The same is applicable to the European Union. The Maastricht Treaty, first, and the Amsterdam Treaty later, while favoring the process of European integration, also represent the concession of the economic sovereignty by the member States.[190] The abolition of customs barriers in the geographic area of the Shengen Agreement corroded territorial sovereignty. The redefinition of the internal organization and of the tasks of NATO, represent a sort of concession of the military sovereignty of each of the member States.[191]

Furthermore, the legislative acts of the European Union are discussed and enacted not by the Parliament, but by the Executive Council.[192] While the former is elected by the people, the latter is composed of personalities appointed by the governments of each member State. The concession of the normative power to a non-elected body represents the yielding of the most important of the sovereignties.[193] Moreover, the directives of the European Union become immediately effective in the member nations,[194] which can be brought to trial for not immediately having them executed.

Just recently[195] the Italian Constitutional Court, in pronouncing on the admissibility of several popular referenda,[196] has found two questions inadmissible, because, if successful, they would have abrogated laws which, although enacted before the creation of the Union, would have hampered the correct execution of successive European directives.[197]

Having completed the stage of the integration process which has been characterized by inter-governmental accords, the debate then concentrated on defining a Charter of Fundamental Rights and Liberties of the European People, postponing, once again, to a more remote future the goal of a political Constitution of the Union.[198]

The necessarily slow "transformation" from the rigid system of Civil Law to the more flexible Common Law system, represents the unconscious assent of the whole nation to Fundamental Charter of the European people.

The nation has been able to seize the modifications which have taken place in the "material" Constitution and has come to realize that any future attempt to amend the "written" Constitution will have to begin from the modifications occurred, and not from the letter of the 1948 fundamental law. But this is not yet equivalent to saying that the material Constitution, made of constitutional praxis and conventions, while being "original," is identifiable with the constituent power.[199]

The modifications, as substantial as they have been, in the relationship among constitutional organs and the shifts of competence, seem to be going in the direction of the assumption of a constituent power by each of these organs. It is this evolutive process which makes of Italy a European laboratory that attracts the interest even of foreign scholars.[200]

## NOTES

1. The parliamentary system was chosen by the Constituent Assembly and sanctioned in Article 94 of the Constitution of 1948.

2. M.E. de Franciscis "Constitutional Revisions in Italy. The Amending Process", in Paolo Janni (editor), *Italy in Transition: the Long Road from the First to the Second Republic* (Washington, D.C.: The Council for Research n Values and Philosophy, 1998), pages 44-48.

3. Italian Constitution, Article 94 "The government must have the confidence of both houses".

4. This phenomenon has been known as *partitocrazia* and has been discussed by the international scholarly community for the last twenty years. For all, see Joseph La Palombara, *Democracy Italian style* (New Haven: Yale University Press, 1987); and *Political Science Quarterly*, special Issue: *Presidential and Parliamentary Democracies: Which Works Best?* Vol. 109, n.3.

5. In 1994 in fact a new electoral law was approved by Parliament, which established that 75 percent of each House would be elected with the majority system while the remaining 25 percent would be attributed to the political parties, proportionally to the votes expressed by the people and provided they received more than 4.5 percent.

6. The new electoral law increased the perception that each voter could "make the difference" and thus modified the relationship between voter and elected representative, reducing the relevance of the political parties as *trait d'union* between the people and the government.

7. To name just the most recent changes at the European level, the Maastricht and Amsterdam Agreements and the treaty creating the Shengen area.

8. S. Labriola, *Storia della Costituzione Italiana* (Napoli: Edizioni Scientifiche Italiane, 1995).

9. "Albertine Statute", Article 2: "The State is governed by a Representative Monarchical Government".

10. *Ibid.*, Article 5: "He is the Supreme Head of State".

11. *Ibid.*, Article 3: "The legislative powers shall be exercised collectively by the King and two Chambers: the Senate and the Chamber of Deputies".

12. *Ibid.*, Article 5.

13. *Ibid.*, Article 6.

14. *Ibid.*, Article 9.

15. *Ibid.*, Article 7.

16. *Ibid.*, Article 8.

17. At the time of the proclamation of the Kingdom of Italy and until 1881 the *criterium* for enjoying the right to vote was based on real estate and personal wealth. Between 1882 and 1911, there was a mixed system by which the level of wealth was lowered while literacy was introduced.

18. In 1912 a law turned the suffrage universal, or so it is called, although women were still excluded and only men over 30 years of age are admitted to vote. Real universal suffrage was introduced in Italy after 1945, when men and women of age 21 were admitted to vote. In 1975 the legal age to exercise the right to vote was further lowered to 18 for both sexes.

19. The *non expedit* was issued by Pope Pius IX in 1868, prohibiting Italian Catholics from participating in electoral politics. It was later enforced in 1874, ordering Catholics not to exercise either active or passive political rights. It was partially relaxed in 1912, allowing Catholics (on limited grounds and with severe restrictions established in a pact known as the Patto Gentiloni) to participate in the first "universal suffrage" election in 1913. For

more on this subject, see, M.E. de Franciscis, *Italy and the Vatican: The 1984 Concordat between Church and State* (New York: Peter Lang Publishing, 1989), pages 15-52.

20. It is, however, the contention of this paper that the 1948 constitution has not been formally in effect since at least the mid-1980s.

21. Italian Constitution, Article 94: "The government must have the confidence of both Houses".

22. This was done since the legislative branch is the only organ of the State which is directly elected by the people. By being responsible to Parliament, individually and collectively, the Council of Ministers is indirectly responsible to the people to whom "Sovereignty belongs. . . ." Italian Constitution, Article 1.

23. Articles 67 of the *Grundgesetz* sanctions, in fact, the *Konstruktive Mistrauensvotum* by which "The Bundestag may express a vote of no confidence only when it elects by a majority of its members a successor and when it asks the Federal President to withdraw the powers to the Federal Chancellor. The federal President must conform to the requests and appoint the elected. Between the motion and the election must pass forty-eight hours."

24. The only exception to this was the vote of no confidence voted by the Parliament to then President of the Council of Ministers, *Romano Prodi*, October 1998.

25. Italian Constitution, Article 94, comma 5.

26. G. Pasquino, "The Election of the Tenth President of the Italian Republic" in *Journal of Modern Italian Studies*, Vol.4, n. 3, Fall 1999, pages 405-415.

27. Italian Constitution, Article 5 "The Republic . . . implements . . . the fullest measure of administrative decentralization" and Title V, Articles 114-133 are the sources for the proposals and demands of the new "federalist" Italy.

28. The XIIIth Legislature began in 1996 and is expected to end in 2001.

29. The Constituent Assembly did not deem it safe for the democratic regime which had just been established in Italy to sanction the possibility for the people to propose a referendum, so that only the abrogative form was contemplated: "A popular referendum shall be held to abrogate, totally or partially, a law . . . when requested by five hundred thousand electors," Italian

Constitution, Article 75.

30. It includes provisions for administrative transparency which is enforced by instituting a sort of local *ombudsman* called "*difensore civico*".

31. In most cases it has brought the people closer to the institutions, breaking a custom of indifference.

32. Italian Constitution, Article 67 "Each member of Parliament represents the Nation and carries out his duties without constraints of mandate".

33. 83 percent of those who voted did so in favor of abrogating the law. Of further interest is the fact that the same question, asked in the 1993 *referendum*, had been found inadmissible by the Constitutional Court only two years earlier, a sign that the transition was on.

34. *Supra*, footnote 5.

35. M.E. de Franciscis, "Constitutional Revisions in Italy," *cit.*, page 50.

36. Italian Constitution, Article 138 "Constitutional laws shall be adopted by each House after two successive debates at intervals of not less than three months, and shall be approved by an absolute majority of the members of each House in the second voting."

37. Constitutional law 1/1997, Article 4, mandated that a *referendum* be held within three months from the final vote in the last House, notwithstanding the *quorum* reached by the Houses at final vote. For more on the subject see, de Franciscis, M.E. "Constitutional Revisions", *cit.*, pages 48-53.

38. The creation of these authorities, and their "permanent" character, has been considered an important element in favor of the theory of the "transition". For all see, Silvano Labriola (ed.) *Le Autorità indipendenti: da fattori evolutivi ad elementi della transizione nel diritto pubblico italiano* (Milano: Giuffrè, 1999), pages 1-62.

39. These are, just to name a few: the Authority on the Media; the Authority on Free Competition in the Markets; the Authority on Stock Exchange; the Authority on Privacy, and the Authority on Telecommunications.

40. This law amended in part Article 121, and fully Articles 122, 123 and 126 of the 1948 Constitution.

41. The people's discontent with perfect bicameralism and the lack of a true regional chamber has been voiced most loudly by the *Lega Nord*.

42. S. Labriola, "*Il Caso Tedesco*" in AAVV, *Il Decentramento politico negli Stati dell'Unione Europea* (Maggioli Editore, 1997), pages 27-74.

43. G. Duranti, "*Il Caso Spagnolo*" in AAVV, *Il Decentramento politico negli Stati dell'Unione Europea, cit.*, pages 75-109.

44. Constitutional Law number 2/1999 of November 23, 1999 introduced the amendment to Article 111, "Rules on Jurisdiction".

45. Italian Constitution, Articles 13 through 28.

46. The Regional delegates enjoy the same prerogatives had by Parliamentarians. They do not need to be elected members of the Regional Councils, and they are chosen in a manner in which the minorities will be represented. This has meant that at least one of the three delegates is always a representative of the minority political forces.

47. Italian Constitution, Article 83: "The President of the Republic is elected by Parliament in joint session of its members. Three delegates from every region elected by the Regional Council, so as to ensure that minorities are represented, shall participate in the election. Valle d'Aosta has one delegate only".

48. In the last fifteen years many have noted that this very small delegation for each Region does not truly integrate Parliament, rather that the 58 delegates who join in the joint secession represent only symbolically and solely in a secondary manner the decentralization process provided for by the Constitution. For all see, F. Cuocolo. *Principi di Diritto Costituzionale* (Milano, 1966).

49. Italian Constitution, Article 85, comma 2: "Thirty days before the expiration of the term, the President of the Chamber of Deputies shall summon a joint session of parliament and the regional delegates to elect the new President of the Republic."

50. Italian Constitution, Article 83, comma 3: "The election of the President of the Republic is by secret ballot with a majority of two thirds of the assembly. After the third ballot an absolute majority is sufficient."

51. S. Labriola, *Lezioni di Diritto Costituzionale: L'ordinamento repubblicano* (Rimini, 1997).

52. United States Constitution, Article 2,section 1: "The electors shall meet in their respective States. . . . And they shall make a list of all the persons voted for, . . . The person having the greatest number of votes shall be the President, if such number be a majority of the whole number of Electors appointed; and if there be more than one . . . and have an equal number of votes, then the House . . . shall immediately choose by ballot one of them for President." This provision has been superseded by Amendment 12.

53. Which does not mean that the election of the President has always gone peacefully with one agreed upon candidate.

54. This "guarantee" became mute when the electoral law was modified, and fractured multipartitism began changing towards a bi-polar system.

55. Italian Constitution, Article 83, comma 3.

56. S. Labriola, "*Lezioni di Diritto Costituzionale,*" *cit.*

57. G. Pasquino "*The election of the tenth President of the Italian Republic,*" *cit.*

58. M.E. de Franciscis, "*Electing the President: Italian Style*" in *Presidential Studies Quarterly*, Vol. XVI, n.3, Summer 1986, pages 451-459.

59. G.Pasquino "*The election of the tenth President of the Italian Republic*" *cit.*

60. Italian Constitution, Article 84, comma 1: "*Any citizen who has completed fifty years of age and enjoys civil and political rights can be elected President of the Republic.*".

61. Italian Constitution, Article 84, comma 2: "The office of President of the Republic is incompatible with any other office.".

62. Italian Constitution, Article 84, comma 3: "Compensation and endowments of the President are established by law.".

63. He held the executive power from April 1993 to May 1994. The circumstances of this appointment shall be discussed later in this paper.

64. He held that ministry from May 1996 to 1999. During that time he contributed much for the successful entry of Italy in the Euro.

65. Italian Constitution, Article 85, comma 1 "The President of the Republic is elected for seven years."

66. Italian Constitution, Article 60, as amended by Article 3 of Constitutional Law n.2, of 9 February 1963, reads: "The Chamber of Deputies and the Senate of the Republic are elected for five years. The term for each House cannot be extended except by law and only in cases of war." Until then the elections to the Chamber and to the Senate occurred respectively every five and seven years, with the election of the President of the Republic falling in between.

67. T. Martinez, *Diritto Costituzionale*. VIIIE ed. (Milano, 1994), p. 528.

68. Never, except in 1999, was the chance of a second term almost a possibility. However, because of Oscar Luigi Scalfaro's interpretation of the presidential powers, a strong and outspoken opposition to his candidacy came from the leaders of the Polo while a mute hostility came from the hard core of the Olive Tree and Prodi's supporters. G. Pasquino "T"he election of the tenth President of the Italian Republic," *cit.*, p. 408.

69. S. Labriola, *Lezioni di Diritto Costituzionale*, *cit.*

70. Such as the extraordinary convening of the Houses. Italian Constitution, Article 62, comma 2 "Each House may be convened in extraordinary session on the initiative of its President or of the President of the Republic."

71. Such as nominating the President of the Council of Ministers. Italian Constitution, Article 92, comma 2.

72. Italian Constitution, Article 87, comma 10: The President of the Republic "presides over the High Council of the Judiciary".

73. Italian Constitution, Article 87, comma 5: The President of the Republic "*promulgates laws*"; and Article 73 "Laws are promulgated by the President of the Republic".

74. Italian Constitution, Article 74, comma 1: "The President of the Republic, before promulgating a law, may request of the Houses in a message outlining his motives, a new debate."

75. Italian Constitution, Article 59, comma 2 "The President of the Republic may nominate Senators for life five citizens."

76. It is the government who appoints the President and

the Councilmen of the Court of Accounts, or the President of the Council of State, yet these appointments become effective only upon the issuing of a decree by the President of the Republic.

77. Italian Constitution, Article 87, comma 5 "He issues decrees having the force of law and regulations."

78. The *controfirma* — litterally translated, counter -- signature — is the act by which a minister, by co-signing with the President of the Republic assumes the full political responsibility of that decision.

79. Italian Constitution, Articles 87, 59, 62, 74, 88, 92, 126, 135.

80. The deliberations of the High Council of the Judiciary is one of such occasions.

81. Italian constitution, Art. 87.

82. This power and its effects on the transition will be further analyzed in paragraph 7. a.

83. Against this thesis, see: Fausto Cuocolo, *Principi di Diritto Costituzionale*, pp. 573-74. For the legittimacy of the recourse, albeit in very rare and exceptional cases, Paolo Barile, "*I poteri del Presidente della Repubblica*" in *Rivista Trimestrale di Diritto Pubblico* (1958), p. 295 et ss.

84. Italian Constitution, Article 74 "The President of the Republic, before promulgating a law, may request of the Houses in a message outlining his motives a new debate. If the Houses once more pass the bill, it must be promulgated".

85. For all see, F. Cuocolo, *Principi, cit.*, p. 542.

86. Italian Constitution, Article 75.

87. The Constitution clearly sets a veto to amend the republican form of the State (Article 139) as well as budgetary and fiscal laws, in addition to the laws granting amnesty and free pardons and to those authorizing the President of the Republic to ratify international treatises (Article 75)

88. Among these we certainly include the nomination of the Under-secretaries of State, the extraordinary Commissioners for the Government, as well as the Governor of the Bank of Italy and the hierarchy of the Armed Forces. Aside from their obvious and necessary sympathy with the policies of the executive, these nominees do not have access to administrative recourse.

89. Among these we can identify, for example, the

destination of appointment for the prefects, the proclamation of a new city and its boundaries; the nomination of all those officers whose roles and functions can be implied from the constitution.

90. The President of the Republic has in fact a general capacity to represent the will of the nation, *jus repraesentationis omnimodae*, which allows him to speak for the nation and the government when on an official visit abroad.

91. Italian Constitution, Article 78 "The Houses decide on states of war and confer the necessary powers on the Government".

92. Italian Constitution, Article 11 "Italy rejects war as an instrument of aggression against the freedom of other peoples and as a means for settling international controversies."

93. In this sense see F. Cuocolo, *Principi di Diritto Costituzionale*, p. 559.

94. Hamilton, *The Federalist*, number 69.

95. M.E. de Franciscis, "Judicial Misconduct in Italy" in Mary L. Volcansek, M.E. de Franciscis and Jacqueline Lucienne Lafon, *Judicial Misconduct: A Cross-national Comparison* (Miami: University Press of Florida, 1996), pp. 49-66.

96. A. Pizzorusso, *Sistema Istituzionale del Diritto Pubblico Italiano* (Napoli: Novene Editore, 1988), pp. 282-83.

97. S. Labriola, *Il Presidente della Repubblica* (Padova, Cedam, 1986); S. Bartole, "*Il Potere Giudiziario*" in G. Amato and A. Barbera (eds), *Manuale di Diritto Pubblico* (Bologna, Il Mulino, 1984), pp. 642-46.

98. A. Pizzorusso, "*Poteri del CSM e Potere del Presidente del CSM circa la formazione e la modificazione dell'ordine del giorno delle sedute*" in *Questione Giustizia* (1985): 727.

99. Albertine Statute, Article 8 "The King may grant pardons and commute punishments".

100. When a constitutional law amended the original intent of the Constituent Assembly. Constitutional law n. 1, March 6, 1992.

101. Italian Constitution, Article 79 as amended in 1992, now reads "Amnesties and pardons are granted by a law approved by two thirds of the members of each house, both voting the bill article by article and its final and complete version."

102. Italian Constitution, Article 88, in its original version

read "The President of the Republic can, having consulted their respective Presidents, dissolve the Houses or any one of them. He may not exercise this privilege in the last six months of his mandate"

103. This final clause was added through an amendment by Article 1 of the constitutional law, November 4, 1991, number 1.

104. *Infra*, paragraph 7.

105. If this could be, indeed, a possibility, then this too can be included among those situations which could presumably be considered as votes of confidence, and therefore introduce in the Italian parliamentary system a sort of political responsibility for the President of the Republic.

106. *Infra*, paragraph 6.

107. Italian Constitution, Articles 114-133.

108. Constitutional Law number 1, November 22, 1999.

109. This is not the place to enter into this subject, suffice to say here that the new regional governments are more like their counterparts in Germany and in the United States of America than they ever were intended to be by the Constituent Assembly.

110. It can no longer occur because of the impossibility to form a majority, since the electoral law has been changed to introduce the majority rule and the direct election of the presiding officers.

111. L. Paladin, *Diritto Costituzionale* (Padova, 1991), pages 461-476.

112. For more on the nature of this power, see, *infra*, paragraph 7.

113. F. Cuocolo, *Principi, cit.*, page 571.

114. T. Martinez, *Diritto Costituzionale*, VIIIE ed. (Milano, 1994), page 425.

115. S. Labriola, *Lezioni, cit.*, page 375.

116. Italian Constitution, Article 62 "Each House may be convened in extraordinary session on the initiative of its President or of the President of the Republic. . . . When one House is convened in extraordinary session, the other is convened by right."

117. Italian Constitution, Article 135 "The Constitutional Court shall be composed of fifteen judges, a third nominated by the President of the Republic, a third by Parliament in joint sitting and a third by the ordinary and administrative supreme courts.".

118. This has been the case until recently when President Cossiga's appointments were clearly political rather than on merit either in the judicial field or among the scholarly community.

119. Italian Constitution, Article 59.2 "The President of the Republic may nominate senators for live five citizens who have brought honor to the Fatherland through their outstanding achievements in social, scientific, artistic and literary fields.".

120. The Constitutional Court pronounced itself in the sense that every President has this option which is an option and not a mandatory provision established by the Constitution.

121. Italian Constitution, Article 74.2 "If the Houses once more pass the bill, it must be promulgated.".

122. C. Mortati, *La Costituzione in senso materiale*, Ristampa inalterata con una premessa di G. Zagrebelsky (Milano, 1998), pp. 206-208.

123. G. Cuomo, *I poteri del Presidente della Repubblica nella risoluzione delle crisi di Governo* (Napoli, 1962), pp. 27-28.

124. S. Labriola, *Lezioni, cit.*, p. 355

125. This can be readily noticed throughout the minutes of the Constituent Assembly.

126. G. Cuomo, *Lezioni di Diritto Costituzionale Italiano e Comparato: le Libertà Civili* (Napoli, 1977), pages 63-101.

127. S. Labriola, *Storia, cit.*, pages 196-202 and 286-287.

128. G. Guarino, *Due anni di esperienza costituzionale italiana*, in Rassegna di Diritto Pubblico, 1946 now re-printed in *Dalla Costituzione all'Unione Europea (del fare diritto per cinquanta anni)* Napoli, vol. I, 1994, pages 14-17.

129. This is the referendum in which the Italian people voted to put an end to the monarchical experience and to establish a Republic.

130. P. Biscaretti di Cuffia, *Le attribuzioni del Presidente della Repubblica*, in *Rivista Trimestrale di Diritto Pubblico* (1963), p. 267.

131. "Albertine Statute", Article 5.

132. The President of the Republic is defined "*viva vox constitutionis*" by P. Calamandrei, *Scritti e Discorsi politici*

(Firenze, 1966).

133. W. Bagehot, *The British Constitution* (Bologna, 1995, reprint), pages 69-85.

134. S. Labriola, *Il Presidente della Repubblica* (Padova, 1986), p.17.

135. *Infra*, paragraph 5.

136. It is this set of powers which should have negated the "neutral" role of the President of the Republic from the beginning. In this sense, see S. Labriola, *Il Presidente, cit.*, p.7.

137. Italian Constitution, Article 87.

138. Italian Constitution, Article 89.

139. T. Martinez, *Diritto Costituzionale, cit.*, p. 538.

140. L. Paladin, in <Presidente della Repubblica> in *Enciclopedia del Diritto*, XXXV (Milano, 1986).

141. This is a message not foreseen and thus not sanctioned in the Constitution. It differs from the message enumerated in Article 89, since it is not sent (rather it is delivered) and not countersigned. On the juridical nature of this message see, T. Martinez, *cit.*, p. 536.

142. Although some significant symptoms can be found already in the preceding seven year term.

143. F. Cuocolo, Principi, *cit.*, p. 576.

144. The message in question was sent on 26 June 1991. With it, the President invited the Houses to hold a debate on institutional reforms and to set a timetable for these to be implemented in order to keep steering the country in a democratic direction.

145. Chamber of Deputies, *Giuramento e Messaggio del Presidente della Repubblica* (Segretariato Generale, May, 1999), pages 9-10.

146. L. Paladin, *Diritto Costituzionale* (Padova, 1991), p. 465.

147. G. Motzo, *Il potere presidenziale di esternazione e di messaggio*, in *Archivio Giuridico* (1957), 20.

148. S. Labriola, *Lezioni, cit.*, pages 359-360.

149. G. D'Orazio, *Sul "nuovo corso" delle esternazioni presidenziali (1978-1982)* in *Rivista Trimestrale di Diritto Pubblico* (1983), page 429 and ss..

150. C. Fusaro, *Scalfaro e la transizione: non ha fatto*

*quello che poteva*, in *Quaderni Costituzionali* (1999), pages 396-400.

151. It is the political authority by which the President of the Republic exercises the powers granted to him by the Constitution which, along with the discretion by which he makes recourse to them, have increased the personification of the presidential powers. The influence of the mass media and the personal ability to "communicate" have contributed a great deal to the increased prestige and of the Head of State.
F. Cuocolo, *Principi, cit.*, pages 541-542.

152. As pointed out earlier, the President of the Republic is not elected by the people and is not politically responsible. For more on this subject, S. Labriola, *Lezioni, cit.*, pages 354-358.

153. Italian Constitution, Article 92.

154. L. Paladin, *Diritto Costituzionale, cit.*, pages 461-476.

155. Italian Constitution, Article 94 "The Government must have the confidence of both Houses. Each House grants or withdraws its confidence through a reasoned motion, which is voted on by roll-call."

156. Throughout the Republican experience there have been a few instances when the appointing by the President of the Republic was not agreeable to Parliament. This occurred for the eighth De Gasperi government in 1953; for the first Fanfani in 1954; for the first and fifth Andreotti governments in 1972 and 1979; and for Fanfani's sixth in 1987.

157. Presidents Gronchi, Pertini, Cossiga and Scalfaro are the Heads of State who have given the widest and most comprehensive reading of their mandate.

158. Gabriella Duranti, "*Il Governo Tecnico della Transizione*" in *La Transizione Repubblicana*, Atti di una giornata di studio in onore di Giuseppe Cuomo, Padova, 2000, in corso di stampa.

159. *Supra*, paragraph 6.

160. By this term Italians underline the non-political origin of the members of the government. The executive, composed of a majority of technicians, is called "technical government". This kind of government is totally unknown to the Constitution, and it has developed into a tool of last resort in order to avoid dismissing

Parliament and, by so doing, giving the political parties a truce.

161. Ciampi was appointed in order to "ferry" the nation from "the old to the new" system, and, in fact, his government has been called "technical government of the transition". For more see, Gabriella Duranti, "*Il Governo Tecnico della Transizione*" .

162. 1995-1996.

163. President Scalfaro refused the resignations, and the government was prolonged for a short while.

164. Fanfani was nominated because he had expressed the willingness to countersign the act of dissolution.

165. For all, see, S. Labriola, "*<Ritorno alla Costituzione> o mutamenti taciti? Il caso del potere presidenziale di nomina dei ministri*" in *Quaderni Costituzionali*, a. XIV, n.1, aprile 1994, pages 27-51.

166. Italian Constitution, Article 88 "The President of the republic . . . may dissolve Parliament or even only one House."

167. G. Guarino, *Lo Scioglimento delle Assemblee Parlamentari,* (ristampa) (Napoli, 1999), p. 25.

168. G. Guarino, *ibid.*, pages 29-42.

169. This is the electoral reform which introduced the quasi majoritarian system and thus it was foreseeable that the balance of the political parties within the Houses would have shifted. S. Labriola, *Lezioni, cit.*, page 363.

170. Since 1963, when the life of both Houses was made the same, this provision of the Constitution has no practical purpose and thus no President of the Republic has made recourse to it.

171. Even though the decision of the President must be countersigned, in this case the executive accepts the will of the Head of State.

172. In 1994 and in 1996.

173. In 1995, 1997 and in 1998.

174. In 1993.

175. C. Fusaro, *cit.*, page 397.

176. T. Martinez, *cit.*, page 541.

177. This dissolution is also known as dissolution/ punishment.

178. The electoral law, while being an ordinary law, can be called law with constitutional relevance, since it carries major changes on the powers and on the balance thereof among the

constitutional institutions. S. Labriola, *Lezioni, cit.*, pages 248-250.

179. G.Guarino, "*Il Presidente della Repubblica Italiana*" in *Rivista Trimestrale di Diritto Pubblico* (1951), now re-printed in *Dalla Costituzione all'Unione Europea, cit.*, pages 309-398.

180. G. Cuomo, *Il Presidente della Repubblica: Impedimento e Supplenza* (Napoli, 1982), page 21.

181. P. Barile, *I Poteri del Presidente della Repubblica*, in *Rivista Trimestrale di Diritto Pubblico* (1958).

182. Usually the outbursting event is the introduction of a new electoral law, and that is why scholars unanimously agree at dating the inception of the transition in 1993, that is to say at the time of the introduction of the quasi-majoritarian electoral law. See, for all, S.Labriola, *Storia della Costituzione, cit.*, pages 196-202 and 286-287..

183. The thesis of some scholars who see in the first months of President Ciampi a clear sign of a return to a neuter role of the President of the Republic does not seem accentable. More time is needed in order to verify.

184. Italian Constitution, Article 138 "Laws amending the constitution and other constitutional laws shall be adopted by each House after two successive debates at intervals of not less than three months, and shall be approved by an absolute majority of the members of each House in the second voting.". For a more detailed discussion of the procedure sanctioned by article 138, see, M.E. de Franciscis, "*Constitutional Revisions in Italy*", *cit.*

185. J.L. Sundquist, *The Decline and Resurgence of Congress* (Washington,D.C.: The Brookings Institution, 1981).

186. A case for unconscious and not intentional cross-fertilization was already in act with the judiciary, whereas judges in Civil Law countries are always less "*la bouche de la loi*" and more and more "creators, interpreters and reformers" while judges in Common Law countries are conversely becoming more and more "*la bouche de la loi*". M.L. Volcansek, "The Common Law Crosses the Channel and Invades the Continent," paper presented at the meeting *The Legacy of the Common Law*, London, July 18-20, 1999.

187. R. Santi, *Principi di diritto costituzionale generale*

(Milano, 1947).

188. By conditioned sovereignty is intended a sovereignty relinquished, either voluntarily or forcefully, to a super-national organization.

189. M.E. de Franciscis, "Federalism in the United States: Sovereignty vs. Autonomy" in Atti del Convegno *Regionalismo e Federalismo dall'Italia all' Europa*, published in, <1989> *Rivista di Diritto Pubblico e Scienze Politiche*, Anno IV, n. 3-4/1994, pages 779-801.

190. G. Guarino, *Verso l'Europa: Ovvero la fine della politica* (Milano, 1997).

191. This often has occurred in open contradiction with the letter of the 1948 Constitution. To name but one example, compare the Italian military intervention in Kossovo and Article 11 of the Constitution "Italy rejects war as an instrument of aggression against the freedom of other peoples and as a means for the settlement of international disputes."

192. These are the Directives of the European Union which are automatically accepted as internal law. without the control and approval by local Parliaments as it occurs in the case of the ratification of international treatises.

193. And one which the Italian Constitution has clearly vetoed as it can be read in Article 76 "The exercise of the legislative function may not be delegated to the Government."

194. Contrary to the procedure adopted for the ratification of international treatises, *ex* Article 80 Parliament is not required to check upon the content and approve of it for the directive to became effective. Italian Constitution, Article 80 "The Houses authorize by law the ratification of international treaties which are of a political nature . . . or which entail changes to legislation."

195. Opinions 31 through 51 rendered on February 3, 2000.

196. Italian Constitution, Article 75.

197. In particular, the three opinions rendered were n. 31, n. 41, and n. 45.

198. G.F. Ciaurro, "*Verso una Costituzione Europea?*" in <1989> *Rivista di Diritto Pubblico e Scienze Politiche*, 1999, pages 743-751.

199. C. Mortati, *La Costituzione in senso materiale, cit.*,

page 120.

200. M.E. de Franciscis, "The Legacy of the Common Law" in *Rassegna Parlamentare*, Anno XLII, n.1, 2000, pages 121-126.

Table 1
Italian Constitution

**TITLE II**
**The President of the Republic**

Art. 83. The President of the Republic is elected by Parliament in joint session of its members.
Three delegates from every region elected by the Regional Council so as to ensure that minorities are represented shall participate in the election. Valle d'Aosta has one delegate only.
The election of the President of the Republic is by secret ballot with a majority of two thirds of the assembly. After the third ballot an absolute majority is sufficient.

Art. 84. Any citizen who has completed fifty-years of age and enjoys civil and political rights can be elected President of the Republic.
The office of President of the Republic is incompatible with any other office.
Compensation and endowments of the President are established by law.

Art. 85. The President of the Republic is elected for seven years.
Thirty days before the expiration of the term, the president of the Chamber of Deputies shall summon a joint session of Parliament and the regional delegates to elect the new president of the Republic.
If the Houses are dissolved, or there is less than three months to their dissolution, the election shall take place within fifteen days of the meeting of the new Houses.
In the intervening time the powers of the President elect are prolonged.

Art. 86. The functions of the President of the Republic, in all cases in which he cannot carry them out, shall be exercised by the President of the Senate.
In cases of permanent impediment or death or resignation of the President of the Republic, the President of the Chamber of Deputies shall call an election of a new President of the Republic within fifteen days, except for the longer term provided for if the Houses are dissolved or have less than three months to their dissolution.

Art. 87. The President of the Republic is the head of the State and represents national unity.
He may sent messages to the Houses.
He calls elections for the new houses and fixes their first meetings.

He authorizes the presentation to the Houses of draft laws initiated by the government.
He promulgates laws and issues regulations and decrees having the force of law.
He calls popular referendums in those cases provided for by the Constitution.
He nominates in those cases provided for by law the officers of the State.
He accredits and receives diplomatic representations, ratifies international treatises which have, where required, the authorization of the Houses.
He is the commander of the armed forces, presides over the Supreme Council of Defense established by law, makes declarations of war which have been decided by the Chambers.
He presides over the High Council of the Judiciary.
He may grant pardons and commute punishments.
He confers the Honors of the Republic.

Art. 88. The President of the Republic can, having consulted their respective Presidents, dissolve the Houses or any one of them.
He may not exercise this privilege in the last six months of his mandate, unless this period coincides with the last six months of the Legislature.

Art. 89. No act of the President of the Republic is valid if it is not signed by the proposing ministers, who assume responsibility for it.
The acts which have legislative value and those others laid down by law shall be countersigned also by the President of the Council of Ministers.

Art.90. The President of the Republic is not responsible for the acts performed in the exercise of his duties, except for high treason or plots against the Constitution.
In such cases he is impeached by Parliament in joint session, with an absolute majority of its members.

Art.91. The President of the Republic, before entering on his duties, shall take an oath of fidelity to the Republic and to uphold the Constitution before a joint sitting of Parliament.

Table 2.

Electoral "Tickets" in the transition to a Two Party System

| Leader of the Coalition | Election | Coalition Ticket |
|---|---|---|
| Berlusconi | 1994 | FI, AN, LN, CCD, UDC + external support of the Radicals |
| Prodi | 1996 | PDS, PPI, Verdi, UD, Dini + external support of Re-foundation Communists. |

Table 3.
Bicameral Committee's Proposed modifications to the Italian Constitution*

**TITLE II**
**The President of the Republic**

Art.67. The President of the Republic is elected by universal and direct suffrage.

Art.68. The President of the Republic is the Head of State. He represents national unity and guarantees for its independence and integrity.

He makes sure the Constitution is upheld.

He makes sure treatises are honored as well as all the obligations Italy might have because of it being part of international or supra national organizations.

Art.69. The President of the Republic:

a) presides over the Supreme Council for foreign policy and defense, which will be created by a law approved by both Houses, and he is the commander of the armed forces;

b) nominates the Prime Minister, keeping in mind the results of the elections to the Chamber of deputies;

c) upon the proposal of the Prime Minister he shall nominate and remove the other members of the government;

d) he authorizes the presentation to the Houses of draft laws initiated by the government and issues decrees having force of law approved by the Council of ministers;

e) promulgates laws. Before promulgation he may request, in a motivated message, for a new deliberation of the Houses. If the Houses once more pass the bill, it must be promulgated;

f) issues regulations of the Government; he may request a second deliberation. If the Government once more approves it, the regulation must be issued;

g) calls elections for the new Houses and fixes their first meetings;

h) calls popular referendum in those cases provided for by the constitution;

i) sends messages to the Houses and these can generate a debate;

l) declares the war deliberated by the chambers in a joint session;

m) may grant pardons and commute punishments;

n) decrees the appointments in those cases provided for by the Constitution and the law either upon a proposal by the Government or with the consent of the Senate;

o) accredits and receives diplomatic representations, ratifies international treatises, which have, where required, the authorization of the Houses.

Art.70. The president of the Republic is elected for six years. He may be elected for a second term.

Any citizen who has completed forty-years of age and enjoys civil and political rights can be elected President of the Republic. The office is incompatible with any other office and activity both public and private.

The President of the Senate, within ninety days of the expiration of the term, will call for the election which must fall between the sixtieth and thirtieth day before the expiration.

The candidatures may be presented by parliamentarians, by Italian representatives at the European Parliament, by regional councilmen, by provincial presidents and by mayors which must be in the number and according to the terms established by a law approved by both Houses.

The regulations and criteria for the financing of the electoral campaign shall be defined by a law approved by both the Houses, the same shall be done to regulate the participation in television and radio programs so as to guarantee equal opportunity among the candidates.

The candidate who shall have obtained the absolute majority of the votes expressed, shall be the President of the Republic. In the event, no candidate shall obtain the absolute majority, a second ballot between the two highest vote-getters, shall be held within fourteen days from the first election.

The President of the Republic, before entering on his duties, shall take an oath of fidelity to the Republic and to uphold the Constitution before a joint sitting of Parliament.

A law approved by both Houses will regulate the election and will establish all other provisions to fulfill this article.

Art.71. A law approved by both Houses will discipline regulations aimed at eliminating conflicts between private interests of the President of the Republic and public interests.

Compensation and endowments of the President of the Republic are established by law approved by both Houses.

Art.72. The functions of the President of the Republic, in all cases in which he cannot carry them out, shall be exercised by the President of the Senate.

In cases of permanent impediment or death or resignation of the President of the Republic, the President of the Senate shall call an election of a new President of the Republic within ten days. The election must fall on a date within sixty and thirty days after the occurrence of the event.

The permanent impediment of the President of the Republic shall be declared unanimously by a college composed of the President of the Senate, the President of the Chamber of Deputies and by the President of the Constitutional Court.

Art.73. The President of the Republic can, having consulted the

President of the Chamber of deputies and of the Senate of the Republic, call the election of the Chamber of deputies before the ordinary end of the legislature, when the Government presents its resignations as per Article 76 (of the proposed revised constitution). The Chamber of deputies cannot be dissolved during the last six months of the tenure of the President of the Republic. If the natural term expires within those six months, the mandate of the Chamber of deputies shall be extended. The election of the new Chamber of deputies will take place within six months from the election of the President of the Republic.
The Chamber of deputies cannot be dismissed during the six months which follow its election. The term can be extended to twelve months whenever the election has taken place after the election of the President of the Republic.

Art.74. The acts of the President of the Republic, adopted upon proposal of the Prime minister or of a minister shall be countersigned by the proposing party who assumes responsibility for it.

The nomination of the Prime minister, the call for the election of the Chamber of deputies and the dissolution of the same, the call for popular referendum in those cases envisioned by the constitution, the request by a motivating message of a new debate over a law or a regulation, the promulgation of the laws, the messages sent to the Houses, the nominations of members of constitutional organs which are attributed by the constitution to the President of the Republic shall not be countersigned.

Art.75. The President of the Republic is not responsible for the acts performed in the exercise of his duties, except for high treason or plots against the Constitution.
In such cases he is impeached by Parliament in joint session, with an absolute majority of its members.

* The bicameral committee established by constitutional law 1/1997 prepared a draft revision of the second part of the 1948 constitution. Parliament did not vote upon it because it was withdrawned. For a detailed discussion see, M.E. de Franciscis "*Constitutional revisions in Italy, the amending process*" in Paolo Janni (ed) Italy in Transition: the Long Road from the First to the Second Republic, Washington, the Catholic University of America, 1998, pp.43-83.

Table 4.
Constitutional Law 1/ 1999 amending provisions on Decentralization

Art 121. **The organs of the Regions are: the Regional Council, the Regional Executive and its President.**
**The Regional Council shall exercise the legislative powers attributed to the Regions as well as the other functions conferred by the Constitution and the**

**laws. It may submit bills to Parliament.**
The Regional Executive represents the Region, directs the policy-making of the Executive and is responsible for it, promulgates laws and regional statutes, directs the administrative functions delegated to the Regions by the State, in conformity with the instructions of the Government of the Republic.

Art.122. The electoral system and the cases of ineligibility and incompatibility of the President, the other members of the Regional Executive and the Regional councilors shall be established by a regional law in accordance with the fundamental principles established by a law of the Republic, which also establishes the term of elective offices.
No one may belong at the same time to a Regional Council or to a regional executive and to one of the Houses of Parliament, to another Regional Council, or to the European Parliament.
The Council shall elect a President amongst its members and a Bureau.
Regional councilors are not answerable for the opinions expressed and votes cast in the exercise of their functions.
The President of the Regional Executive shall be elected by universal and direct suffrage, unless the regional statute provides otherwise. The elected President shall appoint and dismiss the members of the Executive.

Art.123. Each Region shall have a statute which, in harmony with the Constitution, shall lay down the form of government and basic principles for the organization of the Region and the conduct of its business. The statute shall regulate the right to initiate legislation and promote referenda on the laws and administrative measures of the Region as well as the publication of laws and of regional regulations.
Regional statutes are adopted and amended by the Regional Council with a law approved by an absolute majority of its members, with two subsequent deliberations at an interval of not less than two months. This law does not require the visé of the Government commissioner. The Government of the Republic may submit the constitutional Court within thirty days from their publication.
The statute is submitted to popular referendum if one-fifth of the electors of the Region or one-fifth of the members of the Regional Council so request within three months of its publication. The statute that is submitted to referendum is not promulgated if it is not approved by the majority of valid votes.
Art.126. The Regional Council may be dissolved and the President of the Executive may be removed with a reasoned decree of the President of the Republic in the case of acts in contrast with the Constitution or grave violations of the law. The dissolution or removal may also be decided for reasons of national security. The aforementioned decree is adopted after consultation with a committee of Deputies and Senators for regional affairs, which is set up in the manner established by a law of the Republic.

The Regional Council may adopt a reasoned motion of no confidence against the President of the Executive that is undersigned by at least one-fifth of its members and adopted by roll call vote with an absolute majority of members. The motion may not be debated before three days have elapsed since its introduction.
The adoption of a no confidence motion against a President of the Executive elected by universal and direct suffrage, and the removal, permanent inability, death or voluntary resignation of the Executive and the dissolution of the Council. The same effects are produced by contemporary resignation of the majority of the Council members.

** the sections of Article 121 which have been placed in evidence are the original provisions of the Constitution not having been affected by the amendment.

Table 5.
Constitutional Law 2/1999 amending provisions on "Rules on Jurisdiction"

Art. 111. Jurisdiction is implemented through due process regulated by law.
All court trials are conducted with adversary proceedings and the parties are entitled to equal conditions before an impartial judge in third party position. The law provides for the reasonable duration of trials.
In criminal law trials, the law provides that the alleged offender shall be promptly informed confidentially of the nature and reasons for the charges that are brought and shall have adequate time and conditions to prepare a defense. The defendant shall have the right to cross-examine or to have cross-examined before a judge the persons making accusations and to summon and examine persons for the defense in the same conditions as the prosecution, as well as the right to produce all other evidence in favor of the defense. The defendant is entitled to the assistance of an interpreter in the case that he or she does not speak or understand the language in which the court proceedings are conducted.
In criminal law proceedings, the formation of evidence is based on the principle of adversary hearings. The guilt of the defendant cannot be established on the basis of statements by person who, out of their own free choice, have always voluntarily avoided undergoing cross-examination by the defendant or the defense counsel.
The law regulates the cases in which the formation of evidence does not occur in an adversary proceeding with the consent of the defendant or owing to reasons of ascertained objective impossibility or proven illicit conduct.
**All judicial decisions shall include a statement of reasons.**
**Appeals to the Court of Cassation in cases of violations of the law are always**

**against sentences and against measures affecting personal freedom pronounced by ordinary and special courts. This rule can only be waived in cases of sentences by military tribunals in time of war.**
**Appeals to the Court of Cassation against decisions of the Council of State and the Court of Auditors are permitted only for reasons of jurisdiction.**

** the sections of Article 111 which have been placed in evidence are the original provisions of the Constitution not having been affected by the amendment.

Table 6.
Presidents of the Italian Republic

| *Name* | *Party* | *Ballots* | *Days* | *Tenure* | *Votes* | *Total* | *%* |
|---|---|---|---|---|---|---|---|
| Enrico De Nicola | — | 1 | 1 | June 1946-Dec. 1947 | 405 | 556 | 72.9 |
| Luigi Einaudi | PLI | 4 | 2 | May 1948-May 1955 | 518 | 872 | 59.4 |
| Giovanni Gronchi | DC | 4 | 2 | May 1955-May 1962 | 658 | 833 | 78.9 |
| Antonio Segni | DC | 9 | 5 | May 1962-Dec. 1964 | 443 | 842 | 52.6 |
| Giuseppe Saragat | PSDI | 21 | 13 | Dec. 1964-Dec. 1971 | 646 | 937 | 68.9 |
| Giovanni Leone | DC | 23 | 16 | Dec. 1971-June 1978 | 518 | 996 | 52.0 |
| Sandro Pertini | PSI | 16 | 10 | July 1978-June 1985 | 832 | 995 | 83.6 |
| Francesco Cossiga | DC | 1 | 1 | June 1985-April 1992 | 752 | 977 | 76.6 |
| Oscar Luigi Scalfaro | DC | 16 | 10 | May 1992-May 1999 | 672 | 1014 | 66.3 |
| Carlo Azeglio Ciampi | — | 1 | 1 | May 1999-Present | 707 | 1010 | 71.4 |

Original source: de Franciscis M.E. "Electing the President :Italian Style" in *Presidential Studies Quarterly*, Vol. XVI, n. 3. p.453.

## Table 7.
## The President and the Legislative Branch

- He fixes the first meeting of Parliament (Art.87.3)
- He may convene in extraordinary session Parliament (Art.62.2)
- He ratifies international treaties which have, where required, the authorization of the Houses (Art. 87.8)
- He can dissolve the Houses (Art.88.1)
- He may sent messages to the Houses (Art.87.2)
- He authorizes the presentation to the Houses of draft law initiated by the government (Art.87.4)
- He promulgates the laws (Artt.73.1 and 87.5)

- He may request of the Houses a new debate on a law (Art.74.1)
- He may dissolve town, provincial and regional councils (Art.126.1and Law 142/1990)*

*as modified by Article 4 of constitutional Law 22 November 1999, number 1.

## Table 8.
## The President and the Executive Branch

- He nominates the President of the Council of Ministers and, on his proposal, the Ministers (Art.92.1)
- He nominates the officers of the State (Art.87.7)
- He nominates the Under secretaries of State (*)
- He makes declarations of war, is Commander of the Armed forces, presides over the Supreme Council of defense (Art.87.9)
- He confers citizenship (**)
- He confers the honors of the Republic (Art.87.12)
- He accredits and receives diplomatic representations (Art.87.8)

* as introduced by Law 400/1988
** as established by Law 91/1992

## Table 9.
## The President and the Judiciary

- He presides over the High Council of the Judiciary (art.87.10)
- He nominates one third of the Constitutional Court (art.135.1)
- He grants pardons and reduces jail sentences (art.87.11)

Table 10.
The Composition of Governments
1979-1996*

| *Period* | *President of the Council of Ministers* | *Composition of Governments* |
|---|---|---|
| 4.08.1979-2.04.1980 | Cossiga (I) | DC, PSDI, PLI<br>Abstention of PSI,PRI |
| 4.04.1980-18.10.1980 | Cossiga (II) | DC,PSI.PRI |
| 18.10.1980-28.06.1981 | Forlani (I) | DC, PSI, PSDI, PRI |
| 28.06.1981-23.08.1982 | Spadolini | PRI, DC, PSI, PSDI, PLI |
| 23.08.1982-11.12.1982 | Spadolini (II) | PRI, DC, PSI, PSDI, PLI |
| 11.12.1982-3.08.1983 | Fanfani (V) | DC, PSI, PSDI, PLI<br>Abstention of PRI |
| 4.08.1983-1.08.1986 | Craxi (I) | PSI, DC, PSDI, PRI, PLI |
| 1.08.1986-17.04.1987 | Craxi (II) | PSI, DC, PSDI,PRI, PLI |
| 17.04.1987-28.07.1987 | Fanfani (VI) | DC |
| 04.1994-12.1994 | Berlusconi | FI, AN, LN, CCD,UDC<br>External support of Radicals |
| 18.05.1996-1998 | Prodi | PDS, Ppi, Verdi, UD,Dini<br>External support of RC |

Table 11.
Dissolution of Parliament

| *Legislature* | *Period* | *Duration in Years* | *President* |
|---|---|---|---|
| Fifth | 1968-1972 | 4 | Leone |
| Sixth | 1972-1976 | 4 | Leone |
| Seventh | 1976-1979 | 3 | Pertini |
| Eighth | 1979-1983 | 4 | Pertini |
| Ninth | 1983-1987 | 4 | Cossiga |
| Tenth | 1987-1992 | 4+10 months | Cossiga |
| Eleventh | 1992-1994 | 2 | Scalfaro |
| Twelth | 1994-1996 | 2 | Scalfaro |

## CHAPTER II

# LITERATURE AND SOCIETY IN ITALY

*MARISTELLA DE PANIZZA LORCH*

### A PERSONAL PREMISE

An analysis of the complex relation of Italian literature to society allows me the unexpected pleasure of reopening an intense dialogue. This I shared during my forty American years with many contemporary Italian writers and critics, as well as with men and women from all walks of life. All of whose personal friendship I shall treasure to the end of my days. That dialogue was interrupted when I left the directorship of the Italian Academy for Advanced Studies in America in 1996. I trust that the Italian Academy at Columbia University, built together for the intensification of that particular dialogue, will fulfill its scope in a not too distant future. For me, personally, the dialogue re-opens today.

Eduardo de Filippo, Giuseppe Prezzolini, Giuseppe Ungaretti, Ernesto Grassi, Maria Corti, Alberto Arbasino, Alberto Moravia, Italo Calvino, Antonio Tabucchi, Umberto Eco, Annalisa Cima, Maria Luisa Spaziani, Giovanni Vattimo, Giuliana Morandini, Gianni Riotta are just a few of my longtime Italian writer friends. Among the critics: Giuliano Manacorda in particular; with him, Petrocchi, Bosco, Sansone, Ossola, Branca, D'Amico, Asor Rosa, Padoan, Baratto, Segre, Quondam, Ferroni, Lombardo, Perosa, Massimo Salvadori. Each of these names evokes for me the story of a happy crossing which overcame the separation of Gibraltar and the Atlantic which lay between us.

Many other Italians come to my mind today, too many to mention by name. They were the women and men from different walks of life — artists, professionals, leaders and officials in the political world, diplomats, businessmen, publishers, journalists, shopkeepers and workers of all kinds — whom I met officially or casually in my many tours of Italy during the past fifty years, alone or with my family. Among them I cannot refrain from mentioning a handful of men and women: Annalisa Cima, Maria Fede Caproni,

Dina Vattani, Carla Martella, Marika Bollea; Federico Fellini, Roberto Rossellini and Luchino Visconti; Giulio Andreotti, Francesco Cossiga, Francesco Corrias, Antonio Amato, Antonio Ruberti, Luigi de Nardis and Michele Dipace.

Thanks also to Ambassador Paolo Janni, the most active among the first Guarantors of the Academy, and to the Department of Politics of the Catholic University of America. These dear Italian friends today are all present among us. They are a bridge which strengthens and corroborates *nella realtá effettuale de la cosa*, as Machiavelli would say, the meaning and value of an international agreement Italy signed in 1991 with an important American university. It is not a marriage vow that unites a couple but the need and patiently sustained desire to complement each other through hardships and differences. Our meeting today evidences that "pensare insieme", the motto of the Italian Academy at Columbia, can be successfully realized everywhere in America, beyond a specific Agreement and a particular beautiful building.

Within the Academy itself, I wish to thank the staff for their technical assistance and hospitality and Jenny McPhee, Fellow in Residence and translator of Italian literature, for having enriched my understanding of the ongoing debate on the *noir* novel. The 'contemporary' aspect of literature provided an occasion to meet with young Americans and Italians on the Columbia campus whose familiarity with the contemporary Italian novel has been much more intense than mine. I am thankful also to Oonagh Stransky, writer and translator of prose and poetry. Oonagh translated the excerpts from Arbasino's *Fratelli d'Italia* and the other Italian quotations that appear in the final section of the essay. My thanks to Giuliana Ferrone, a voracious and super-enthusiastic reader of everything Italian, who inspired me to look beyond the close circle of personal acquaintances.

The central part of this essay deals with Dante and Ariosto, whose Poems offer two paradigmatic examples of an ideal relationship of Literature to Society. Had he lived, Italo Calvino would have co-taught a course with me on Ariosto in the "Renaissance Program" at Barnard/Columbia. For the 'contemporary' section, I offer up a collection of notes, gathered from the perusal of my own library, a personal homage to the Italian writers and critics who enriched it.

## THE 'DIVINITY' OF A MEDIEVAL COMEDY

Within the deep transformation that European society and its literature has undergone during the past fifty years, the Italians stand out for the combative spirit with which they greeted, during the years 1943-46, a radical cut with their Fascist past. Evidenced in both theory and practice, Italian neo-realistic film and literature of that period, by boldly identifying the artist's mission at the service of his people, constitute a unique moment of spontaneous encounter of the writer with his 'people,' not to be equaled in the rest of the century. The writer and the artist in general, according to the neo-realistic aesthetic code, should not only reflect with realistic immediacy moods and mainly needs of his society, but should support and lead society in the realization of its needs.

The neo-realistic aesthetic canon is not traditionally Italian. There is, however, an example of 'engagement' or *impegno* at the very origin of Italian literature which deserves our attention. The example is so extraordinary that it precludes imitation.

> When Dante wants to express lightness, . . . no one can do it better than he does, . . . but his real genius lies in the opposite direction . . . in transmitting the sense that the world is organized into a system, an order, a hierarchy where everything has its place. . . . Dante gives solidity even to the most abstract intellectual speculation. (Italo Calvino, *Memos for the Next Millennium* [Cambridge, Mass.: Harvard University Press, 1988])

Columbia takes pride in one college course named "The Great Books". Virgil, Lucretius, Ovid, Horace, Livy and Tacitus, Augustine, Dante, Ariosto, Machiavelli, Galileo — authors within the Latin-Italian tradition — have provided me with my daily bread during my half century of life as an American. They convinced me that every book that survives through the centuries, that is, very `good' book (a term I prefer to `great') or those we read more than once lives a life of its own. The `contemporary character' of such a book is defined by its power to speak to us today, no matter when and where its author lived. In the case of a so-called `Great' or `good book,' author and book live together as an indissoluble unity. This implies that the author survives somehow within that `immortal' book as a human being living in time and space, in a specific historical moment and place. The contemporary nature of a `great book' is to be found in the universality of the theme dealt with, not in the abstract but in the *hinc* and *nunc* of the society within which the author lived. From these obvious and rather banal premises, we may conclude that, generally speaking, literature and society are indissolubily connected, if not always, then at least in special moments of man's History.

Yet, these miraculous moments of 'Grace' are explained only partially by 'particular events' in the life of a given society, such as a great war, a revolution, a famine, a political upheaval. I personally side with those who, in the much debated issue, believe that the miracle takes place by force of exceptional Human Beings who reflect the life of their society not directly, like an historian, but through a 'poetic' Myth or Fable of their creation.

Italian Literature opens with such a miracle. The *Divine Comedy* so clearly proves the point as to make me hesitate to bring it to your attention. Italian received its baptism as a literary language with a story whose author takes himself, together with his 'society,' on a pilgrimage through Hell, Purgatory and Paradise; it starts with a poem in 100 cantos of 120 lines each, in the words of its author "*a cui han posto mano e cielo e terra,*" to which heaven and earth contributed. The *Comedia* was in fact so perfect in this unusual combination of the human and the divine that Boccaccio, an Italian poet and writer who lived a generation after Dante, called it "divine", read it in public and wrote one of the first commentaries on it. Its spirituality is based on the concrete of human experience and a 'system' based on it. Its 'weight', in Calvino's terms, does not mess on the part of the poet a magic use of 'lightness'. Dante seems, in fact, to be one of those rare poets who can render the exact weight of lightness, as in "*come di neve in alpe senza vento*" (Inf.XV), and in "*come per acqua cupa cosa grave*" (Pd. III, 123), snow falling on a mountain without wind, a heavy object falling in dark water: weight and lightness, body and soul, human and divine.

What is divine about the *Comedia* is something Boccaccio,

who was an instinctively sharp critic of poetry, perhaps intuited and therefore implied. Its 'divinity' — I dare argue — makes it today the Italian book most popular in America, the Italian book which enjoys every year a steadily increasing number of translations. The *Comedia* is undoubtedly the most contemporary of all Italian books because of the harmonious coexistence within it of the absolute and the relative, the universal, and the particular, what man can perceive and enjoy under any sky and in any time, and the very personal connection with Dante's own 'world' or society and not necessarily ours.

"Dante's World" was the title of a very popular course at Barnard and Columbia which I introduced in the early 70's— immediately after the Columbia riots — with the participation of the medieval historian, Susan Wemple, the theologian Ewert Cousins, translator of Bonaventure's "*Itinerarium mentis in deum*" and the art historian, Howard Davis, a specialist on Giotto. "Dante's World" stood at the center of a "Program in Medieval and Renaissance Studies" which we officially inaugurated in 1976 with a generous grant from NEH. Umberto Eco, a medievalist whose doctoral dissertation deals with Saint Thomas's esthetics, presented in that course "*Il nome della rosa*" before it was translated into English.

What prompted us four colleagues to join hands for one course was the very 'divinity' of the *Comedia*, defined above as its contemporaneity. How can one hold a class of fifty American students for three or four hours prisoners of the luminous heavens of Dante's *Paradiso* if the poet, by virtue of his art had not accomplished the miracle of transforming the theology and the astronomy of his own time into a 'vision' that lives like his Empyreon beyond time and space? Although, however, we were, all four colleagues in the course, convinced of the miracle accomplished by Dante as poet, we felt the students should become aware of Dante as a human being within the historical background, in all of its ramification, in which the miracle took place.

Dante held our students spellbound — as they listened to his poetry in the original, I must add — not because he is a saint or a life model, but because he is a man/poet whose poem was born out of his very human experience. He lived the problems of his own society with an extra-ordinary perceptiveness and intensity, not necessarily with historical objectivity. Dante accomplishes the miracle of universalizing the reality of his own personal life and society as a human being conditioned by the human body within which he breathes. The *Comedia* lives of this paradoxical reality.

From the very first Cantos the reader learns that Dante is an exceptional human being with a tremendous faith in God and in himself; he is God's creature as a poet, the two being inextricably interwoven. Dante is so convinced of being the 'Chosen One' as to discourage , at the threshold of paradiso, those readers who cannot identify with his mission from following his boat into an ocean that nobody has faced before or will ever face after him:

*O voi che siete in piccioletta barca*
*desiderosi d'ascoltar, seguiti*
*dietro al mio legno che cantando varca*
*tornate a riveder li vostri liti. . . .*
*L'acqua ch'io prendo gia mai non si corse*
*Minerva spira, e conducemi Apollo.*

O you that are in your little bark, eager to hear, following behind my ship that singing makes her way, turn back to see again your shores. . . . The water which I take was never coursed before. Minerva breathes and Apollo guides me. (Singleton)

Then he adds:

*Voi altri pochi che drizzaste il collo*
*per tempo al pan delli angeli . . .*
*metter potete ben per l'alto sale*
*vostro navigio, servando mio solco*
*dinanzi all'acqua che ritorna equale* (Pd. II, 1-15).

You other few who lifted up your necks betimes for bread of angels . . . you may indeed commit your vessel to the deep brine, holding to my furrow ahead of the water that turns smooth again. (Singleton)

Paradise is the kingdom of light. Yet, the Light of which paradise is made, expression of God's glory, is darkened by the constant shadow of a misled humanity on earth that daringly attempts to efface such glory. Dante conceives of, and portrays humanity in the most detailed concreteness of his own personal life, of his own society, of his own city, the Florence he loves and detests. In the very heart of paradise, the most powerful invectives against a Pope that misleads humanity involve Florence, the Poet's sweet nest. There he was born and grew to be a man; there he hopes to return someday honored with the laurel crown he earned as a poet. High up in paradisiacal space, in the Heaven of the Fixed Stars, Dante expresses this hope with a sudden tragic sense of certainty which disconcerts us. The canto was composed in 132O, one year before the Poet's death in exile, in a moment in which he drew hope from the historical condition in Italy and Florence:

> *Se mai continga che 'l poema sacro*
> *al quale ha posto mano e cielo e terra*
> *sí che m'ha fatto per piu'anni macro,*
> *vinca la crudeltà che fuor mi serra*
> *del bello ovile ov'io dormi' agnello*
> *nemico ai lupi che li danno guerra;*
> *con altra voce omai con altro vello*
> *ritornero'poeta, ed in sul fonte*
> *del mio battesmo prendero' il cappello.*
> (PD XXV, 1-9)

> If ever it come to pass that the sacred poem to which heaven and earth have so set hand that it has made me lean for many years should overcome the cruelty which bars me from the fair sheepfold where I slept as a lamb, an enemy to wolves which was on it, with changed voice now and with changed fleece a poet I will return, and at the font of my baptism I will take the crown. (Singleton)

The *Comedia*, which marks the birth of Italian literature, is at first sight a powerful indictment of the society in which the Poet lived. The Poet speaks not for himself, but in the name of

God for the people who suffer under leaders who are unaware that individual human life on earth is nothing but 'a running towards death':

> "*Tu nota,*" says Beatrice to his beloved in the unreal light of Earthly Paradise, "*e come da me son porte,/ cosi queste parole segna ai vivi/ del vivere ch'e'un correre alla morte*". (PG. XXXIII, 52-4)
>
> Do write down (in your memory) and as they are said by me, reveal these words to the living of a life which is a rapid run to death. (Lorch)

Here in a nutshell is the case of the divine comedy. At the threshold of the 14th century, Dante Alighieri, socially-speaking a modest Florentine poet, boldly declares: God has chosen me, a Florentine poet, to experience the other world. God himself engaged me to write down that experience by memory, so as to warn the misleading leaders of humanity of the impending divine intervention to re-establish order within a humanly-created chaos. The poet speaks for and to his own Florence, as well as to the people of the world as *Vox Dei*. By living it as real, he believes the very myth on which the poem is based and which is unbelievable by human reason.

The *Comedia* stands like a lonely rock in a desert. Unreachable and therefore inimitable. Dante creates a language but does not establish a tradition of deeply committed literature. Popular in Italy through the XIV century, the *Comedia* was almost immediately eclipsed by Petrarch's *Canzoniere* and its imitators, and later by the revival of ancient Rome during the Renaissance. Dante re-emerged only four centuries later, not by merit of the Italians but of the German and English Romanticists, as the most forceful expression of the rediscovered Middle Ages.

A poetic myth, even as forceful as Dante's *Comedia*, carried within itself the characteristics and tastes of a society antithetical to, and therefore rejected by, a differently oriented society. Dante's moral, religious and political engagement did not appeal for centuries to the literary world of Italy, because it was for centuries alien to the taste of Italian society. If asked, I guess Calvino would say that the Italians incline to the 'light'.

## RENAISSANCE HUMANISM AND THE MYTH OF FOLLY AND INSANITY IN ARIOSTO'S *ORLANDO FURIOSO*

> We might say that throughout the centuries two opposite tendencies have competed in literature. One tries to make language a weightless element that hovers above things, like a cloud, or better perhaps the finest dust, or, better still, a field of magnetic impulses. The other tries to give language the weight, density and concreteness of things, bodies and sensations. . . . We should be unable to appreciate the lightness of language if we could not appreciate language that has some weight to it. . . . Lightness for me goes with precision and determination, not with vagueness and the haphazard. (I. Calvino)

An epoch, like an individual, has its own unique way to express its essence and identity. The *Comedia* proves by its very contemporaneity that poetic myth expresses forcefully, in a way different from history, the essence of Medieval society in crisis. Two centuries after Dante, during the Italian Renaissance, which was wrongly defined by some 19th century historians as the triumph of 'Art for Art Sake', two leading poems, the *Orlando innamorato* and the *Orlando furioso*, closely mirror, through their fantastic tales of labyrinthine adventures, the essence of an era we define today as "Renaissance Humanism".

'Lightness', Calvino would say, characterizes the two poems of fantastic adventures in contrast with the 'weight' of the *Comedia*; the lightness, however, is not obtained at the expense of precision and determination. The precision of images, as well as the masterly use of irony within the world of adventures created by Boiardo and Ariosto, is a direct reflection of a society permeated with the philological and rhetorical ideals of a militant kind of humanism which climaxed in Italy during the second half of the

15th century. It takes 'lightness' to convey through literature a feeling for such a complex and in many ways contradictory period in the history of Italian society as the phenomenon in question.[1]

A myth which centers on the folly of Orlando, the wisest and the most popular Paladin of Charlemagne — the very popular Italian version of "Roland" of the *Chanson des gestes* — is the leading motif of the *Orlando innamorato* and of the first half of the *Orlando furioso* (up to Canto 23). Only folly, as freedom of the senses and of the imagination defeating all conventions, can explain as expression of extreme vitality, the most passionate, all encompassing, doubly sinful, unrequited love of the wisest and strongest Christian warrior for Angelica, an Oriental Muslim princess. In spite of its sinfulness and unconventionality, this love spurs Orlando to the most daring adventures. With him the best Christian knights and Muslim heroes all lost in their love for Angelica.

The myth of Orlando's folly reflects in its extraordinary irrepressible vitality the mood of the society to which Boiardo and Ariosto belonged. Orlando's *immenso vigor*, the leading motif of the *Innamorato* and of the first half of the *Orlando furioso* constitutes in this sense a homage to the greatness of an era in which philology was born as the discovery of the revealing power of Literature, the key to the affirmation of Man in history. The era of erudition and of its limitless value; of a godlike drive for life, not in contrast, but in harmony with a new concept of Christianity; of the liberating power of laughter, which triumphs particularly in Pulci's poem *Morgante*; of the constructive force of *diletto*; of *docta ignorantia* and *coincidentia oppositorum*. *Tout court*, it was the era of folly. Erasmus composed the first version of his "In Praise of Folly" after a visit to Italy in 1512!

At the end of the 15th and the beginning of the 16th century, the Dutchy of Ferrara, seat of the Court of Este, where the two poets lived and wrote as courtiers and refined humanists, offers the ideal background and inspiration for a society of *literati*, most of them very practical men, involved in the politics of their time, all inspired by the highest humanistic values.

At the time Boiardo was working at the *Orlando innamorato* Ferrara had enjoyed almost 50 years of 'golden peace', during which art and letters thrived and a free exchange of ideas was enjoyed at its best throughout the peninsula without limits or borders. The *literati* like the bankers, were citizens of the world. Debates on ideas of this very special *res publica literarum* had given birth to a new literary genre, the dialogue which was realistic at least in appearance.

A century before Ariosto, the daring humanist, Lorenzo Valla, founded 'philology' in the "*Elegantiae Latinae linguae*" and 'history' based on philologically credible documents in the "*De falso credita donatione constantiniana.*" He vigorously upheld in his dialogue "On Pleasure as the True Good" man's godlike drive for earthly sensual pleasure as the source of life. The dialogue was composed by a very young Lorenzo at the court of Pope Martin V. Later it was revised by him as a teacher at the universities of Pavia and Milan. It was finally completed at the court of Alphonse of Aragon in Naples before Valla returned to Rome in charge of translations from the Greek at the Vatican Library. Valla had not only boldly defined the basic drive for life as *voluptas*, or sensual pleasure, but with the support of the Bible and of Saint Paul developed it into love of and for God, source of all kinds of goods for man to enjoy. Voluptas'/'utilitas', pleasure/ expedient, was proved by Valla to be the basic Christian virtue, antithetical to '*honestas*' the pagan (Ciceronian) virtue for virtue's sake.

In his dialogue, *De Voluptate ac de Vero bono* (1421-44, Rome, Pavia, Milan, Naples, Rome), Valla attempted to give a daring philological justification to sensual pleasure as the origin and source of life. This eloquently interprets a curiosity, widely experienced in Italy, for life on earth in all its aspects. It is this new intense form of 'curiosity' that leads Italian society to exploit the discovery of classical antiquity as a new model and inspiration for a fuller life on earth, as well as to face with a new enthusiasm the challenge of the new geographical, scientific and artistic frontiers. With the humanistic dialogue there triumphed a new form of thinking and visualizing reality. This inspired both the *Innamorato* and the *Furioso*, and in Ariosto found its most daring and well-rounded expression.[2]

Ariosto goes one step further than Boiardo in the interpretation of *Amor omnia vincit improbus*. The positive creative force of 'folly', precisely in the middle of the Poem (Canto

23), transgresses into insanity, a subhuman state in which man — in this case, the great Orlando — loses his identity. It is 'folly,' as life's creative spirit, however, in the first half of the poem, that allows us to enjoy a vision and extraordinary portrayal of human passions parallel to society's discovery of a world within man.

Ariosto's poetic interplay, within the myth he invents, of 'folly' and 'insanity' betrays the Poet's awareness of the dramatic historical change that took place in the world around him after Boiardo's death in 1494. The year 1494 marks, with the descent of the French King Charles VIII into Italy, the first of a series of catastrophic events.

The tale of Orlando's folly, before the hero is overcome by insanity, can be understood in itself as the most comprehensive metaphor of life a poet could conceive. Within this metaphor, *la gran follia* or Orlando's insanity presupposes a development to the limits of Orlando's positive *follia*, his greatness in love, in arms, in life, the great humanity, tout court, of the opening of man's inner life. Orlando's positive *follia* should be read as a homage the poet pays to the discoveries and ideals of a 'humanistic' society of which he is the product, insanity should be interpreted as the mythical version of the dismay for its tragic ending, caused in great part by almost thirty years of bloody fighting the poet Ariosto witnessed in part at least with his own eyes.

With the end in 1509 — year of the first publication of the *Furioso* — of the so called "Herculean peace", an epoch abruptly ends for Ferrara. During the next three years the city and its poet are hurled into one war after the other. In 1508 the League of Cambrai had allied Emperor Maximilian and King Louis XII of France against the Venetians for the partition of the territory of the Republic. The League ends in 1510, setting Pope Julius II free to try to expell the French from Italy. Alfonso, Duke of Este, is at the side of the French, providing with his two famous guns, Gran Diavolo and Terremoto, the best part of their artillery. Fighting takes place all over around Ferrara. The Pope now proclaims The Holy League with Venice and Spain against the French and Ferrara — which, by the way, had been for centuries a fief of the Vatican. The Duke of Este and General Bayard cut to pieces the Papal forces. In 1511 the Spaniards and the Papal Army enter the territory of Ferrara. Yet, the young French General Gaston de Foix moves triumphantly from one victory to the next. Joined by Alfonso's powerful artillery, Gaston de Foix fights on Easter Sunday , April 11, 1512, the bloodiest battle fought on Italian soil since the overthrow of the Goths: the battle of Ravenna, a city a short distance from Ferrara. The dead included 4,000 Frenchmen and 10,000 confederates; all Spanish and Papal leaders are captured. Gaston de Foix is killed when the fighting is almost over. Alfonso's artillery is a decisive factor in the final victory, as well as in the cruel death of thousands of people. When the fighting is over, he tries in vain to restrain the French from committing atrocities against the unarmed people of Ravenna.

The poet Ariosto openly condemns such atrocities in the first person at the opening of a canto in the 1516 version of his poem. He witnessed, against his own will — since he was by nature 'a lover of tranquilities' — many of these events as he physically stood near Alfonso, against his will courtier and 'servant' of the defiant Duke. As a poet, he takes his revenge by carving out for himself a space at the opening of each canto — a couple of octaves — within which he expresses his own view on human passions as well as, at times, on contemporary events. It is however through the myth of Orlando's Folly degenerating into insanity, that he succeeds in making those tragic events as permanent as they were originally vivid.

The treaties of Cateau Cambresis, some twenty years after Ariosto's death, brought, with Emperor Charles V, a definitive peace to the peninsula. With peace came the end of the independence of most Italian states. Ferrara will survive under the Dukes of Este until the end of the century when the Pope will finally reclaim it as his possession.

Ariosto lived long enough (he died in 1532) to see the end of the harsh fighting. The final development of Orlando's myth may be read as reflecting a serene acceptance of the new political equilibrium established under Emperor Charles V. Orlando, who acted through 16 cantos as a brute deprived of reason, finally regains sanity in Canto 39, five cantos before the closing of the story. Orlando's recovery of his *senno* by will of God, specifically in order to assure the victory of the Christians in the final duel against the Muslims (42), evidences a remarkable optimism on the part of the poet, an optimism in spite of all odds, an adaptability and a resilience which I am tempted to define as typical of Italian society in general, not uniquely of 16th century Italy.

I am tempted also to relate, by contrast, what I call Ariosto's final 'optimistic' solution in the development of his hero Orlando to the deeply pessimistic view of a Northern society which is evidenced by the contemporary Poem, *Narrenschiff.* Brandt's *Ship of Fools*, published in 1494, stands at the threshold of German literature as a strong pillar of Reason and social order, a nostalgic longing for the old order, described in word and image as chaos through the shipwreck of the historically real 'boat of the insane' or 'ship of fools'.

In contrast with Brandt, Ariosto's agile and fluid development of his myth from folly to insanity to a kind of miraculous recovery of reason by divine intervention is made possible by Ariosto's masterly use of 'literature', that is by his capacity of molding to his heart's content that kind of 'lightness' of language which Calvino describes as one of the two opposite tendencies in literature;

> One tries to make language into a weightless element that hovers above things like a cloud, or, better, perhaps, the finest dust, or better still, a field of magnetic impulses. (Calvino, *Six Memos* . . ., p. 15)

Ariosto's 'lightness' of language is to be identified mainly with his all pervading use of irony, in the development of the plot of the poem, as well as within the individual stories. As light as Dante's magic butterfly 'that flies towards justice without impediments' (Pg. X), Ariosto's irony untangles the world he creates free from the worm of the 'real'. Not darting straight upwards like Dante's, but flittering from flower to flower, irony follows and permeates in the *Furioso* the uninterrupted wandering of its knights into a borderless world of forests, mountains, plains and islands, their duels and love making, their fantastic battles in which horses and men inextricably intermingle like in a painting of Paolo Uccello. Irony transforms the real into a magic world that exploits the earth to the maximum by including the moon as part of it, together with new islands, continents and underground miraculous realms. At the very center of this magic world is man as the poet sees him, spurred into living by his passions and desires, so greedy of life as hardly to listen to the voice of reason. Irony imbues the whole of the poem, transforming it into something 'else,' as does a snowfall to a familiar landscape.

Irony permeates from beginning to end the episode of Orlando's re-acquired mental sanity. The most foolish of the Christian warriors, the English Astolfo, recovers the hero's *senno* (reason) in a huge flask among discarded objects, by flying to the moon on the Ippogrifo, a winged horse. Subsequently, helped by some friendly Paladins, Astolfo chains the giant brute Orlando — after having properly washed him — to the Atlas Mountains. Finally, Orlando is forced to breathe in the content of the flask. What the poet gives us in the end is the old Orlando, the one we have never known in the Italian literary tradition, the Paladin devoted to the Cause of God and Emperor, who will, indeed, contribute to its final victory. But 'Reason,' alas, has deprived our hero of the creative charge of Folly's imagination! Ariosto's final message regarding the fate of his hero Orlando is ambiguous to say the least, as ambiguous, perhaps, as his opinion of the political developments he witnesses in Italian society .

Ariosto acquires his 'lightness' of language often in the wake of Dante's 'weight'. Analogies and differences can be discovered at times in Ariosto's use of a Dantesque image, a word, a metaphor. This is the case of the word/image/metaphor *selva,* forest.

The first image we meet as we open the *Comedy* is the one of a dark forest in which the poet/pilgrim is lost:

> Nel mezzo del camin di nostra vita/mi ritrovai per una selva oscura/che la diritta via era smarrita.

> Midway in the journey of our life, I found myself in a dark wood for the straight way was lost. (Singleton)

What the poet Virgil offers Dante is a way out of that dark forest, not directly but through a long deviation that includes Hell and Purgatory. The allegory of Dante's forest is transparent: the moral and psychological confusion that cuts the poet/pilgrim off from the Light of God.

Like Dante's *Comedy*, Ariosto's poem is written in the first person. The poet, however, is not a pilgrim in search of personal salvation but a storyteller who entertains his fellow courtiers with the product of his imagination, the fantastic adventures of the mythical Italianized Orlando. While the *Comedy* proceeds on a straight line, focusing on Dante as the main character, the *Orlando Furioso* moves on by continuous digressions, offering the view of a thick forest, an intricate interplay of adventures by a great number of knights who endlessly wander through a mythical world covering the whole planet and beyond. Orlando's story of folly and insanity is but one thread of the multicolored cloth.

Under a certain aspect the *Furioso* could be read as the parody of the *Comedy*, which it definitely is not. The most constructive and enjoyable way to read it is actually in relation with the *Comedy* as the reflection of a moment in the history of Italian society which is as much plurivocal and rich in contradictions as Dante's is univocal.

Realism triumphs in the description of the phenomenon of insanity itself, in its physicality, of the stages one by one that a human psyche undergoes when in prey of this terrible illness, until a human being, no matter how noble and strong, totally loses all contacts with the world around him. Without *senno* action lacks motivation and purpose. Orlando, insane, can be explained only like the eruption of a volcano, a flood, an earthquake.

At the threshold of the second section of his Poem (Canto 24, 1-3), immediately after the description of Orlando's painful entrance into darkness, Ariosto stops to meditate for a moment on the nature of *pazzia*, insanity, which he conceives of as a human deviation from the road of sanity. The poet humanist's main interest is not the pursuit of spiritual happiness, but serenity of soul. This is obtained within an Epicurean/human rather than a Christian/religious context. Here in the description of *pazzia* or insanity, he echoes Dante's language. The loss of reason, in consequence of unrequited love leads man into a great forest, *una gran selva* where one is bound to get irremediably lost, no matter how much one tries to find a way out. That forest is a prison where one is forever chained down, without hope of escape:

*Varii gli effetti son, ma la pazzia*
*e 'tutt'una pero che li fa uscire.*
*Gli e' come UNA GRAN SELVA, ove la via*
*convien a forza a chi vi va fallire:*
*chi su' chi giu', chi qua', chi la' travia.*
*Per concludere insomma, io vi vo dire*
*a chi in amor s'invecchia, ogn'altra pena*
*si convengono i ceppi e la catena.* (XXIV, 2)

The various effects which from love spring
By one same madness are brought into play.
It is a wood of error, menacing,
Where travelers perforce must lose their way;
One here, one there, it comes to the same thing.
To sum the matter up, then, I would say:
Who in old age the dupe of love remains
Deserving is of fetters and of chains. (Reynolds)

The ironic twist to which Ariosto submits the Dantesque metaphor of *selva* — echo in more than one instance Dante's episode of the unfortunate lovers Paolo and Francesca. It is reinforced by the poet's following personal confession, carried out tongue in cheek in the first person. The poet would personally like to free himself from the chains of physical sensual love, but he cannot do so because the illness has reached the bones: "*ma tosto far come vorrei non posso/che'l male e' penetrato infin all'osso.*" "And yet I fear my vow I cannot keep: In me the malady has gone too deep" (Reynolds).

Is Ariosto using the metaphor of *selva* for insanity or for 'life' itself in general, human life as he sees it is prey of passions and desires? Is this a confession of frustration on the part of a humanist who lives 'free' of the many constrictions to which Dante and his society were subjected, or rather an acceptance of a *de facto* condition which has its advantages? It is hard to tell. There are very few moments in which Ariosto seriously means what he says. One instance of tough seriousness, indeed anger, is the episode of Ebuda — an addition of the last, 1532 version of the poem — in which Orlando pronounces a curse against firearms —

*l'archebugio* — by throwing the satanic invention into the ocean. What evokes the poet's unconditional condemnation is an inhuman deviation of society around him, a threat for human survival. For the rest we are left to guess.

Dante singles himself out within the society in which he lives. Victim of his own society, he seeks and finds justice and harmony by appealing to eternal principles above humanity. Ariosto, a man among men, shares the good and the bad of his own society. Through the arm they have in common, the use of language in literature, Dante condemns while Ariosto smiles at human weaknesses and sins and at the deviations of his own society.

## NOTES ON LITERATURE AND SOCIETY IN CONTEMPORARY ITALY: A NOVEL; A GENRE; DEBATES 1945-2000; THE PROFILE OF AN AUTHOR

### *A Novel*

From Arbasino's *Fratelli d'Italia* (1969-1993) (Milano, Adelphi, 1993):

> *Da noi, si agita Antonio, in questo momento sono denunciati o sotto processo Testori, Pasolini, Visconti, Antonioni, mi pare anche Fellini, e parecchi altri che non ricordo, tra i quali parecchi astuti che fanno in fretta un romanzo con un titolo equivoco e un poco di porcate nelle prime pagine, le sole che il magistrato di solito legge. . . . Tutti ben scritti, tutti brillantini, tutti uguali . . .perfettamente traducibili, coi falsi problemi moderni di una coppia molto moderna in vacanza tra l'autoroute e la Riviera in mezzo a ragazzine tutte uguali alle attricette . . . vanno sempre bene . . . grandi puttanate . . . solo esercizi, collages di parole in pagine come pezze di tweed . . . e mai un'opera compiuta, mai LE LIVRE! come se un pittore o un musicista producessero solo schizzi e abbozzi e 'appunti per.'* (pp. 92-3)

"In our country," Antonio says agitatedly, "they're accusing and prosecuting people like Testori, Pasolini, Visconti, Antonioni — Fellini too, I think, as well as many others whose names I can't remember, bright people who churn out books, give them provocative titles, throw in a couple of raunchy scenes in the first few pages — the only pages the judges actually read . . . they're all well written, all quite brilliant, all the same, perfectly translatable, with their false modern day problems — a modern couple on vacation, caught somewhere between the highway and the Riviera, surrounded by girls that look like young actresses . . . it always works . . . all gimmicks . . . they're only exercises, really, just collages of words woven together like tweeds . . . there's never a completed work, never Le Livre! It's as if a painter or a musician were to produce only sketches or drafts or 'Notes for'."

*Cosi raccontiamola anche a questo, al ristorante Margana, la vecchia storia degli anni di guerra passati sentendo i bombardamenti di la dal confine. . . .* (p. 197)

And so, while sitting at the Ristorante Morgana, we tell him, too, the same old story of how we spent the war years listening to bombs dropping on the other side of the border.

*Il Romanzo, all 'osteria! . . . a cercar padron migliori. . . .* (p. 95)

The Novel, to the tavern! . . . to find a better host.

*Se poi il tema di un tuo romanzo o di un tuo film fosse come sempre la Fine di un Mondo? o di una societa', o di una civilta' o di una cultura . . .?* (p. 94)

And what if your film or your novel were always about the end of a world? Or the end of a society or of a civilization or a culture . . . ?

*"La fine di un'epoca!" come sigla e formula di successo. . . .* (p. 1342)

"The end of an Era!" as the mark of, and formula for, success.

*Il romanzo tradizionale, invecchiato come le pensioni con clientela interessante. Ordine, cautela, assenatezza, rispettabilita', decoro. . . . Garanzie: il Passato assicura l'Immobilità..la Morte accerta che tutto é gia' successo, nulla puo' cambiare, ci si puo' dar pace; l'imperfetto stabilisce l'atmosfera; il Filtro della Memoria regola il passaggio a senso inico di materiali preselezionati, senza imprevisti ne 'turbative.*

*Due periodi ben distinti: fino a un certo punto si e' tentato di vivere; dopo si e' cominciato a scrivere* " (p. 1343).

The traditional novel, like a run-down pension with its "interesting" clientele. Orderliness, prudence, common sense, respectability, decorum. . . . Guaranteed: the Past assures Fixedness. . . . Death ascertains that everything has already happened, that nothing can change, that we can leave each other alone; the Imperfect sets the atmosphere, the Filter of Memory regulates the flow of pre-selected material in one direction, with no surprises or disturbances.

Two clearly distinct periods: up until a certain point one attempts to live; then, one begins to write.

*. . . Un Nido di Memorie: tana di nostalgie, cuccia di malinconie, covo di rimpianti. Desiderio di immutabilita'; riordino di dagherrotipi; il paese dei nonni, non un posto nuovo. Vegheggiamento del finito, del gia' conosciuto. Elevazione del concluso, congelamento dello status quo, con manutenzione in economia e un alone 'flou'.*

*Tema fondamentale per tutta la cultura piccolo-borghese: come avendo chissà cosa da rimpiangere e da inorgoglirsi: Sciuscia', Ladri di biciclette, Riso amaro, Fontamara, La Ciociara? L'8 settembre e date analoghe? . . . Nostalgia della provincia sentimentale e crepuscolare, nella letteratura a successo. Vagheggiamento per il Rinascimento, nella regia antiquaria e gentilizia.. Costumi e mobilio. Magazzini e deposito.* (p. 1343)

A nest of Memories: warren of yearnings, lair of sorrows, cove of regrets. Desire for constants; the immutability of things; the reorganization of daguerrotypes; the land of our grandparents; no new places. The longing for endings, for the already known. The elevation of conclusions, the congealing of the status quo, thriftiness and a blurred halo.

Basic theme for the culture of the petit bourgeois: having something to mourn, something to be proud of: Sciusciá, Ladri di Biciclette, Riso Amaro, Fontamara, La Ciociara? What about the 8th of September, and other such dates? Nostalgia for the sentimental and crepuscular aspects of the provincial, as in the major literature. Courting the Renaissance with antiquated and heraldic stagings . . . costumes and furnishings, warehouses and storage areas.

*La riproduzione della lingua parlata . . . Ma insomma come sara' stata la conversazione italiana in un paese che (secondo la sua letteratura) e' sempre stato impacciato o muto?* (p. 1350)

The reproduction of the spoken language . . . now really: what can spoken Italian have been like — in a country (as depicted by its literature) of awkward and embarrassed silences?

*Non soltanto le persone: anche le epoche hanno un loro modo riservato, scaltro e frivolo insieme di comunicare il proprio io piu'profondo a qualcuno che coglie al volo le confidenze piu' sorprendenti di un secolo spossato e vicino alla morte come un altro Swann . . . dando a una societa, a un momento storico la possibilita' di raccontare le proprie memorie. . . .* (p. 1368)

Not just people: epochs, too, have their hidden ways, simultaneously cunning and frivolous, of communicating their deepest sense of self to one who can grasp the shocking intimacies of a worn out century, close to its death, a Swann. . . . Giving society, giving a historical moment a chance to retell its own memories.

*Ma che non muta l'eta'? Si rivolgono i regni mentre che io canto e si cambiano le mode galanti.*

(*Abbiamo appena ordinato i pomodori al riso*)

What doesn't alter a period? Kingdoms turn against me as I sing, and gallantries change.

(We just ordered tomatoes with rice.)

> *Sento rumore: due o tre gridi, trambusto nel corridoio. Poi bussano forte. Desideria si e' buttata dalla finestra. Scendo le scale di corsa, e il corpo e' davanti alla porta sul marciapiede; lo stanno coprendo adesso. Morta sul colpo battendo la testa. (Tutto da riscrivere qui).*
>
> *Siamo li tutti. Non aveva parlato a nessuno? No. Non ha lasciato scritto qualche cosa? No, niente.* (p.1371, closing statement).
>
> I hear a noise, two or three yells, a scuffle in the hallway. Then they're knocking hard at the door. Desideria threw herself out the window. I run downstairs, the body is in the doorway, on the sidewalk; they're covering it at this very moment. Dead on impact, a blow to the head. (All this has to be rewritten.)
>
> We're all there. She didn't say anything to anyone? No. She didn't leave anything in writing? No, nothing.

Carlo Bo, a veteran of Italian letters, said more than once that everybody in Italy today writes a novel, but very few have something to say. Faced with the challenge of a choice of books to select that may serve the purpose of relating literature to society in Italy, I remind myself that my aim in the present lecture is not to offer you a path in the dark forest of contemporary literature. For that task I am not the most competent person available. Rather, I follow my natural instinct which almost unconsciously leads me towards those books whose authors I have met, towards those critics who have allowed me a personal insight into their way of thinking and a perusal of their books they left in my personal library.

There are two copies of one book in my library, a ponderous novel of 1371 pages, entitled *Fratelli d'Italia.* Each copy has an affectionate dedication by the author. My reaction as I reread the book today, seven years after the publication of its second version, is more positive than ever before. Here is one of the few novels of which it can be said that it truly takes place in contemporary Italy , light and anguishing, happy and tragic, brilliant and dark. It is a novel that deals with the present with a deep almost unconscious awareness of the past. It 'photographs' Italian society as it breathes around its author with such an uninterrupted use of irony as to allow us readers from this shore of the Atlantic ocean a sense of its complexity, rather than of its merits. For discriminating Italians, in my opinion, it is "the Italian novel of the century"; it lashes out while laughing and praises while condemning. It takes into account not only the world of creative writing , of novels (*romanzo*) in particular, but of the lively debates on its nature and mission. These have thrived in Italy since the early 50s, that is, from the birth of the so called 'neorealistic' movement in literature and film after the end of the war and the fall of Fascism. Its author, Alberto Arbasino has been, from beginning to end, a leading figure within those debates, as well as a prolific writer.

The title itself of the novel, *Fratelli d'Italia* (Brothers of Italy) makes us stop and think. Coming from the opening of the Italian National Anthem, the title denounces ironically as fake and void a nationalistic inclination in Italian letters which the book sets out to destroy.

The 1371 page volume I have in hand today constitutes Arbasino's rewriting of a novel he wrote in the 60s, a living echo of the Italian society of the time. The plot is so loose that it can hardly be summarized: the story of a grand tour of Italy by a group of young men and women, Italian, French, German, Antonio, Jean Claude, Klaus, Enrico and many others as they meet in their uninterrupted wandering — a group of young men and women permanently "on the road".

The result of the 1993 re-elaboration of the original is an irreverent and imposing novel which portrays Italian contemporary society in action with incomparable lightness and mobility. What inspires Arbasino to rewrite an old book is his conviction that "literature is not made only of definitive texts. Most of it reveals itself as temporary versions that one can improve by going back to them with the added advantage of new experiences. . . ."

*Tutto libri*, the Italian version of our *New York*

> *Review of Books*, with reference to the new version of *Fratelli d'Italia* — said "Arbasino — it was written in a 1994" is one of the few Italian successful writers because of his immense curiosity in overcoming '*la letteratura da cortile che affligge da sempre il nostro paese*' (the 'neighborhood literature' that forever afflicts our country). He is an Italian writer who acts, speaks and writes like a Frenchman or an Englishman, bending the Italian language and behavioral patterns of Italians to ways foreign to them. Excess of knowledge, of information may hinder the narrative rhythm. Aware of this risk, Arbasino breaks the sentence in two, overcoming the structure based on monologue (of the first version) molding it into a structure marked by intensive dialogue. The result may be fatiguing for the reader. Yet in Arbasino we have the one Italian who consciously breaks with the traditional novel still in use in Italy today, '*un romanzo*', he says, "*invecchiato come le pensioni con clientela interessante*" (like a run-down pension with its 'interesting' clientele). Hence, the co-presence in the new version of narrative and reflection, soul and body, irreverence and real drama. A parody of life. The young men and women who are the protagonists of the story meet, converse, eat, sleep, laugh, admire without really 'existing' because they have apparently used up their existence in an effort to capture everything that the century has produced in ideas, emotions and thought, experiences, fantasies, pain, desire, anguish and miseries. . . .

*Fratelli d'Italia* is an indescribable novel in American terms which we should read. It calls for translation!

Arbasino's *Fratelli d'Italla* reflects with irony a confused echo of ideas and voices in contemporary Italian society as well as in Italian literature and at the same time a longing for something new and different to express a moment of crisis. Among the many genres practiced in Italy today, the most successful, in the sense that it has found a favorable audience in America, judging from the recent translations, is a special kind of detective novel, '*il giallo*', the *noir*.[3]

I shall not attempt here to trace the origins of the genre, but only say what I know about it. At the beginning there was Umberto Eco's *The Name of the Rose*, as an example of a mixed genre, the detective and the historical novel. Was Eco aware that he was inaugurating a genre destined to great success? I doubt it. If one were to ask him, he would dismiss the question as irrelevant. I have in my library one of the first copies of *Il nome della rosa* brought to America. It bears a generous dedication from its author "*da letterato esordiente, timorosissimo*". Eco followed with the apprehension of a '*novellino*' the reception of his first novel in society.

Eco's first novel was successful not because of the genre he chose, but because it is written from beginning to end in limpid, fluid prose and because, within the 'detective', the author, a most serious medievalist, respects the medieval environment in which it takes place — one intense week in 1327, five years after Dante's death.

Most novels by Sciascia are classified as 'detective' and reflect with passion contemporary history. But today's Italians seem to have moved further than Eco and Sciascia. Whereas the detective novel follows a paradigm of clues— my friend Oonagh reminds me of Ginzburg in *Miti, emblemi, spie* — in the *noir* surprises and contradictions beset the plot. The *noir* offers at first sight at least a mimetic interpretation of society. On a deeper level, however, the protagonist lives within a reality that's not based on cause and effect, but formed of compromises. In line with Gianni Vattimo's '*pensiero debole*' all choices, however, are weak ones. The protagonist does not seem to obey any universal law. Violence prevails and overwhelms the reader. The author, on the other hand, may stand aside and philosophize about it. What can we make of it in America today?

It is perhaps this 'philosophizing' that unbalances the American reader. Take the case of Antonio Tabucchi in his recently translated and successful *The Headless Body*. A reviewer in the *Times* on Feb. 20 (Michael Pye, author of *Taking Lives*), definitely likes the book. Yet he remarks as a weakness that

> this Italian academic, professor at the University of Siena, theoretician and translator, does not write the usual type of thriller. Fascinated by Portugal, he follows crimes in Oporto with the precision of a reporter. The result is an exceptionally 'vivid book' but 'for the oddest reasons': the author, obsessed with observing reality with all his senses, focuses on "how theory can possibly relate to literature," how, for example, the literary world connects with someone being tortured. Result: a journalist who makes his living with bloody murders suddenly slams the door on the captive reader and starts a seminar. You may sometimes snort with exasperation and send Tabucchi's book swirling across the room. But then again when did you last find a novel this interesting?

What the American writer resents in his Italian colleague, I surmise, is the art of mixing high and low culture, evil and good, dark humanity and higher ideals: To contaminate the pure *divertissement* of the *noir* with reflections on violence and on the nature of evil.

*A Genre*

A debate on the Italian passion for and against the *noir* is going on at this moment on the Internet, Giuliana Ferrone reminds me. I should follow it. The writer Scalfaro defends the traditional novel as it changes through phases, against the fixedness and superficiality of the *noir*. Isn't the traditional novel dying of its self-inflicted death — the defenders of the *noir* counterattack — because the society on which it is based has become a '*folla vociante di individui anonimi e isolati*'?

A fact universally recognized in the world of letters is that Italy does not traditionally incline towards long narratives as do France, England and Russia. Perhaps the *noir* fits best with the short novel the Italians tend to write. Or is Italian society rejecting the 'intellectualism' of some Italian novels? (Thus runs my discussion with Jenny McPhee.)

Simon Blackburn, Distinguished Professor of Philosophy at the University of North Carolina, in reviewing Eco's latest book (which is certainly not a novel) "Kant and Platypus: Essays on Language and Cognition" in the *New Republic* of February 7, 2000, warns the reader that the "intellectual temperature is here much higher than in the novels. . . . Eco's trademarks are there: high themes, arcane learning, strange corners of philosophy and history and natural history, large intellectual vistas, a sense of play." Yet something is discouraging about this particular book. In reading it one finds oneself running off with the author to the edge of a cliff. Eco refuses to recognize the cliff because "like the platypus he has adapted himself perfectly to an environment, in this case an intellectual environment. But what he has produced should make us worried about that environment, which is much bigger and ubiquitous even than he is."

Eco is one of the intellectuals more deeply connected with a recurrent debate on the issue of engagement or commitment of the writer to the community. Although the reviewer deals here with a collection of essays, not with a novel, by relating this particular work to Eco's novels he suggests that there is an inclination to consider intellectualism characteristic of the contemporary Italian novel. Do intense recurrent intellectual debates interfere in any way with the spontaneity of Italian novelists? Is the *noir* one of the forms of escape from this tendency, while still partakiing of it?

> *E pero' vero che tutto il Novecento e' mosso dalla contraddizione. L'intrecciarsi, l'intersecarsi e il divergere di discorsi (e correnti) su questo nostro secolo vuol dire proprio che esso e' aperto a ogni possibile discorso sulla letteratura, che mai potra' essere esaustivo, allo stesso modo che mai potra' essere esaustivo un discorso sulla realta' e l'uomo contemporanei.* (Giovanni Occhipinti, *L'ultimo Novecento*, Foggia, 1997)
>
> And yet, it is true that the 20th century was spurred by contradictions. Discourses and trends have

intertwined, intersected and deflected in such ways that now any commentary on literature is to be considered valid, the topics will never be exhausted, just as the discourse on reality and contemporary man can never be exhausted.

*Dove sarebbe la mia libertà se*
*non fosse nel libro*
*Se il mio libro non fosse la mia liberta' cosa sarebbe?*
(Edmond Jabes, quoted by Occhipinti)

Where would my freedom be
if not in the book
If my book were not my freedom, what would it be?

*Un concerto indifferenziato.* (R. Luperini)

An indifferentiated concert.

*Ognuno senza trionfalismi e con i mezzi a disposizione se ne va per la sua strada.* (A. Beradinelli)

Each of us, freed of the need to triumph, equipped with our natural means, sets off down his own path.

*Il probema numero uno resta quello di sopravvivere* (G. Majorino)

The major problem is still survival.

*Nulla e' sicuro, ma scrivi* (F. Fortini)

Nothing is sure, so write.

(All quoted by G. Manacorda in *Letteratura italiana d'Oggi*, 1965-85).

*Debates*

Among my Italian documents I most treasure the 1945-46 correspondence Eduardo de Filippo entertained with my then husband, Claude Bove, an officer in the American army in Italy, and myself. Overwhelmed by the first Roman performance of *Napoli Milionaria*, I had introduced Claude to Eduardo and convinced him to translate the play, find a financial backer in New York and launch it on Broadway. Having lived through the tragedy of Naples while in Rome, Eduardo's dramatic interpretation of the war and after-war period in Naples and its rehabilitation of Neapolitan society was, in my opinion, stunning. Kazan liked the play but did not give the final yes for its production on Broadway by William Cowan. "Eduardo's Naples comes too late and too early for our American audience" was his sibylline statement. Dolph Sweet, director of the Barnard Theater, and later an actor in Hollywood, and I performed the first act of *Napoli Milionaria* at Barnard College in November 1951, with actors that were members of the Barnard faculty.

Eduardo de Filippo is for me one of the most vivid examples of the break between the old and the new in Italian literature that characterizes the immediate post-war period. WWII had cut the peninsula in two, brought the end of twenty years of dictatorship, and fed, with the resistance movement against the German occupation, a civil war destined to have serious consequences in the subsequent political formation of democratic Italy. Society calls at this point for a new kind of literature not only to portray its moods and needs, but to speak for the people and support it in its fight for survival. The writers of the *Ventennio* are violently attacked, first and foremost the philosopher Croce and his 1925 "Manifesto" for his defense of an independent art. The call is for literature and art committed *à tout prix*, for '*impegno*' at all cost. Among the writers under fire are Ungaretti, Montale and Moravia.

The attack, seen from this shore of the Atlantic at the distance of fifty years, is as fascinating as the defense carried out at first, among others, by Carlo Bo, today still alive and active in the world of letters. A weakness is admitted by the accused writers, not however a crime. Angiolelli boldly proclaims in the *Fiera letteraria* against Trombadori that art is an individual phenomenon.

As for the popular art of the day, he proclaims it a horror (*che bruttezza*!).

The debate itself as it develops from the 50s to the 90s, from Milan to Sicily, involved most of the writers whose names we know in America from their novels. A summary would illustrate better than any commentary on the subject the vital contribution of the Italians to an understanding of the issue in question. It affords us, as well, an insight into an aspect of Italian society which is often neglected as we look at Italy from this shore of the Ocean: its instinctive deep commitment to the written word.[4]

What we witness in the original post-war polemics, carried out *viva voce* and through a proliferation of journals, is best described as the painful childbirth of a new reality . Vittorini stands in the forefront, inspired in the journal he directs, by a kind of fanatical longing for a truth that allows the committed writer the discovery of a new Italy. Journals proliferate after the call to arms proclaimed by the communist *Rinascita* and the new *Politecnico*. This was born in Milan, as were most of these journals, and destined to survive for a couple of years.

Partly on the footsteps of the old realists, such as Verga or Pirandello, the literary movement that ensued is baptized "neorealism" (in film as well as in literature). From the bird's eye view of contemporary Italian literature over the last half century, one could argue that the terms of the original polemics remain the basis for a proliferation of polemics and corresponding journals that characterize the literary life in Italy for the rest of the century.

Fortunately, parallel to the theoretical debates, and in spite of them, the writers thrive, some born before or during Fascism, some more direct products of the post-war period. They all breathe a new air, joyously investing a new content with a new style. Berto's *Il cielo e' rosso*, Carlo Levi's *Cristo s'e'fermato ad Eboli*, Italo Calvino's *Il sentiero dei fili di ragno*, and Primo Levi's *La tregua* are just the tip of an iceberg. The tragic theme of the war and the magnificent adventure that was for many the Resistance Movement contributes to killing in style as well as in content the hated Fascist imperialism and its false nationalistic rhetoric. Curzio Malaparte's *La pelle* and the skeptical rendition of war in action given in *Kaput* seem to stand a part from the rest: A Neorealism of a special kind, without enthusiasm.

The miracle produced by the war lasted up to the 50s. Calvino's trilogy signaled a search for new themes, a new inspiration and hence a new language and a new style. Gadda's *Quel pasticciaccio di Via Merulana*, an untranslatable novel with its linguistic experiments, is one of the most successful representatives of the period. Many of the old universally recognized writers, such as Ungaretti, Montale, Saba, Moravia, Vittorini, Pavese, Pratolini, while obeying their own inspirations, participate in and adapt to the new trends.

Speaking in general terms, the 60s express disappointment and skepticism, while offering an example of intense creativeness. "From the disappointment of the events rises the sublimation of words", Manacorda comments. Alberto Bevilacqua's "La Califfa" (1964) — paradigmatic, perhaps, of this period — attempts to give in an intense and accentuated visual way a total sense of life, *l'intricata matassa del vivere*. *Il Gattopardo*, the only book by a singular writer — the Sicilian *Principe di Lampedusa* — a sudden bestseller, (1958), transformed by Visconti into a film, reflects forcefully the vanished enthusiasm of the 40s. The individual stands alone and defenseless against the political power.

Parallel to the economic boom that the country experienced between the 1950 and 1960 and the increasingly industrialized production of books there emerged the fragility of the political structures (see Vittorini in the journal *Menabò*). The mission of literature is seen now in anticipating the representation of industrial alienation, and the upcoming liberation from it. The great ideals of the past gone , literature tends also to the vindication of its autonomy, hence to the renunciation of its ethical and political content. Sanguineti, the most provocative representative of one aspect at least of this period, in spite of his original communist faith, favors a new kind of the once condemned '*ermetismo*'. The critic Anceschi, speaking via the old journal *Il Verri* documents these tendencies.

During this period one of the most interesting literary debates centers on the "opera aperta". Arbasino leads a proposal to transform one's diary into a critical account of ideas, which could inspire the novel in its necessary metamorphosis. Eco in his book *Opera aperta* (1962) suggests such structure of the world as to allow the reader an interpretation *ad infinitum* of a given work of art. Guglielmi among others violently reacts: a given work of art proposes one and one only interpretation of reality! Sanguineti attacks the false ideology of refusal and vindicates the historical function of the movement called '*avantgardia*' to which all the above *literati* belong, provided it is filled with an ideology that promotes engagement, which in his case coincides with Marxism.

This particular debate is central to a literary acolyte that goes by the name of "Gruppo 63," which, in its second official Congress in Reggio Emilia (1-3 November, 1964) finally admits that experience itself is more valuable than the impossible theoretical solutions to the problem. Literature, some declare, must recapture contact with reality, with complete disregard of the instruments proposed by traditional culture. Within the violent divergence of opinion, a wise, critical voice comes from foreign observers — the French Wahl, the American Marc Slonim, the German Wagenbach — isn't the "Gruppo 63" risking to become another *Accademia della Crusca*? An ideological commitment of some kind must be considered by all writers! Special attention is given to language (Sanguineti), but is literature a luxury for the few that can afford it?

At the third meeting of the "Gruppo," or of the "Neo-Avangardia," which took place in Palermo in September 1965, in a chorus of discordant voices Eco speaks with the voice of Reason when he asserts that all sort of avantgard groups aspire to tradition. Insane is the avantgard author who writes in order to be never understood. "He writes to break with a given situation, in order to communicate something different." . Even this common sense assertion is booed by many.

The debates of the 60s find an outlet in the *Sessantotto*, the events of '68, which in principle, aim at upheaval of the bourgeois society. The year, defined in Italy as *Anno dei Portenti*, had long repercussions into the decade that follows. Debates on the role of literature versus society move parallel to the political debates on the attitude towards traditional wealth. Flowing from an acute and chronically pathological stage, these debates focus mainly on how to justify the cultural elite in society.

One advantage literature draws from them, in theory at least, is a greater amount of independence. This is the conclusion we can draw from reading the monthly called "Quindici" (Alfredo

Giuliani, June 1967). What poisons the atmosphere, however, is the political orientation of the journal, the position it takes towards a serious international conflict, i.e. Israel/Palestine in 1969. Eco dominates the scene again with an article in which he condemns the occupation of the Milan Triennale (*Dobbiamo vedere chi occupa, che cosa occupa, e in che rapporto sta con la cosa che occupa*). Violently attacked by Sanguineti and Bonino, he answers ironically with an article "*Vietando s'impara*". Eco again faces the basic problem of the relation literature/society: what should an `*operatore di cultura*' do to parallel the strikes of a factory or the protests of the students against the war in Vietnam? The answer is plain: simply write!

The Neo-avantgard proclaims in *Quindici* a new moderate poetic canon: "*Un romanzo sensato . . . e' un romanzo che ha sacrificato al senso il linguaggio.*" (A sensible novel is one that has sacrificed language to substance.) The neo-avantgardistic stereotype is discarded. The basic question focuses on the way intellectuals conduct politics. Here Eco prevails by clarifying what was at the start the poetic canon of the "Gruppo 63": "*non serve comunicare nei modi consueti la volonta di rottura (suonare i piffero alla rivoluzione) ma bisogna rompere i modi stessi della comunicazione. Questa fu la poetica del Gruppo '63.*" (It does not help to communicate the desire for rupture in the usual ways [to blow the fife of revolution]. One must rupture the `ways' of communication. This was the poetic canon of the "Group 63".)What the Group was contesting was not the necessity of political involvement, but the way in which it was carried out by the traditional left. Guglielmi gives the last interpretation of `commitment' or *impegno* by stating that the most meaningful writers in our century in Italy are those "*che non hanno detto nessuna parola piena, ma hanno significato il dramma della letteratura borghese e fatto della metaletteratura. . . .*" The most significant writers are the writers of meta-literature.

The late 70s and the 80s are dominated by the so called '*riflusso*', not only in literature but in every aspect of art, a great tiredness and a deep disillusionment for a failed revolution and for its having given birth to terrorism. Dominant themes are the defense of eternal values, of quiet living. The voices are many. Pasolini was the first in 1971 to denounce from *Nuovi Argomenti* a literary void created by the "*letteratura/negazione*" of the new avantgard and the literature/negation of the rioting students . The many voices are often in dissent one with the other. There are many real as well as apparent contradictions. New journals, such as the *Collettivo*, propose new forms of commitment . The traditional must be revised, rules and forms of crystallization, eliminated. Journals proliferate: e.g., *Quasi, Salvo Imprevisti*, 1975 in Florence. The focus is on the relation of politics to culture with reference to the journal of the 40s *Politecnico*. Reality is always political; pure art is a thing of the past. The concept emerges of 'alternative culture'; authors such as Sciascia participate in the polemics.

A new form of commitment is proposed in Sicily with the creation of the "*Antigruppo 73*", followed by the "*Antigruppo 75*". What counts in literature — they seem to agree — is not language but the tone, the attitude of the writer . Writers must draw from their own experiences and reflect them in a simple and direct style. A new journal is born: "*Impegno 70*," but strong dissent divides its collaborators. The year 1974 sees the birth of still another Journal "*Pianura*" and still others "*Aperti in Squarci*" and "*Altri Termini*". The authors involved speak with nostalgia of the enthusiasm of the 40s. Drawing from the need for literature to reflect the moral and the political, a voice of resignation comes from the Piemontese critic Barberi Squarotti: "*Credo che alla scrittura non resti altro spazio che quello di essere il negativo continuamente dichiarato dell'utilmente detto. . . .*" (To repeatedly declare the negation of what has been usefully said: this is what is left to literature.) For this purpose, irony is an ideal instrument. Irony must act through an overabundant use of rhetorical figures.

"Confusion, the Espresso comments, is a basic happy moment." Towards the 80s the confusion is political, as well as literary, and not exactly 'happy'. In 1978 the kidnapping and murder of Aldo Moro by the Red Brigades cause a showdown of his party, the Cristian Democrats, who refuse to deal with the '*brigatisti*' to save his life; the Mafia infiltrates the political apparatus; Craxi is elected Secretary General of the Socialist Party, Pertini is at the Quirinale. New literary forms cannot alter immobility in politics. The journal "*Anterem*" (Naples) offers the possibility of a moment of reflection. Apathy reigns. "The only answer left to us, declares Piemontese quoting Baudrillard, is theoretical violence not truth." "*Altri termini*" joins in. The problem that Italian literature faces in its effort to survive, while taking into account a necessary form of social and political commitment, is finding a way to overcome some extreme positions of the neo-avantgard movement. What was called for in the 80s and 90s was a positive action which would put an end to the wild theorizing as well as to some neo-realistic and neo-hermeticist positions. A form of commitment was necessary, but without threatening the survival of the written word, especially poetry. "Without poetry nothing can be done". The rescue of poetry seems to be the Leitmotif of *Altri Termini* in particular. In 1975 a volume was published *Zero, testi e antitesti di poesia* an anthology of 15 Italian poets by Cavallo, an initiative picked up by the journal *Colibrì*. At the same time experiments in language reach extremes. A new journal of poetry founded in Milan in 1977 *Niebo*, directed by Milo de Angelis, signals the rejection of all form of compromise that may impede immediacy— an irrational moment of '*dopo l'attesa e prima dell'incontro*'. The inspirers are Rimbaud and Holderlin. Among the many poets the most acclaimed is Valerio Magnelli.

Literary debates do not take place in a literary void. Among the many voices of novelists to be heard during this period is Primo Levi who first wrote two collections of short stories, *Storie naturali* (1966) and *Vizio di forma* (1971), both lamenting the defeat of reason in the use of scientific and technological progress. He established his identity with a book, *Il sistema periodico* (1975), where science is used metaphorically to describe human situations (the Jewish family) or to reminisce on the past of a scholar of chemistry. *La chiave di stella* follows (1978), centering on the life of a worker, and finally *Se non ora quando?* (1982) where Levi acheives the form of the novel although connected with the chronicle of war. Levi gives here credibility and dignity to the "*partigiano*" as the symbol of a humiliated people that fights for his dignity.

Ottiero Ottieri produces through the 70s and the 80s a number of novels of interest, among which *Il campo di concentrazione* (1972), a syncretism of a story, a diary and an investigation. He analyzes the mind of the psychopathic in *Di chi e' la colpa* (1979), and in *Il divertimento* (1984) deals with the fear of growing old.

Particularly dear to me personally are four women, two novelists and two poets: Giuliana Morandini, Francesca Sanvitale, Annalisa Cima and Maria Luisa Spaziani. I followed all four in their writing and introduced them to American audiences. Morandini exploits a theme in which I am interested: her origins (Friuli, Trieste) lead her to deal with the Austro-Hungarian empire (*I cristalli di Vienna*, 1980 and *Caffe' Specchi*, 1983). Sanvitale follows with a highly lyrical style the memory of contested feelings (*Madre e figlie*, 1980). Cima and Spaziani are splendid poets. Each in different ways is connected personally with Montale, but as poets speak with a voice of their own.

Goffredo Parise's *Il padrone* is the best known novel dealing with the human condition within the industrial world. Finally Bevilacqua emerges in the 80s reminiscing with a limpid style on his youth in Parma (*Vita mia*, 1985). Among the many that come to my mind, I wish to mention Enzo Siciliano, collaborator of CISE (Barnard/Columbia 1980-1990) in the translation of one issue of the journal *Nuovi Argomenti* dedicated to Moravia (1988). In *La notte matrigna* of 1975, Siciliano deals with Nazi Germany and Italy during and after the war. In the *Diamante* (1984), he takes us to a contemporary Calabria in prey of fear. Elegance of style and language are Siciliano's constant preoccupation.

In closing I cannot avoid reporting a sudden change of direction by the Italian Left which inspired Asor Rosa, in the 1982 introduction to the first volume of the history of literature which he edited *Letteratura, testo, società*.

Asor Rosa was for ten years my direct partner in exchanges with CISE, which I founded and directed at Barnard/Columbia between 1980 and 1990. Among the many acts of collaboration, he brought two of his students to Columbia, both became wellknown scholars, Quondam and Ferroni. Asor Rosa, for years a recognized intellectual of the Left, polemicizes in his introduction with two famous critics of the past who stood for an Italian literature of commitment: Francesco de Sanctis and Antonio Gramsci. Asor Rosa refuses to accept two of their basic premises: Italian literature as associated with the ethical and civic history of the country and that the origins of great literature stem from a great moral life. Of course, he admits the obvious: the writer cannot draw his inspiration from literature, that is literature is not born by parthenogenesis. Objecting to the long predominant historical, as well as the structuralist and semiotic orientations, Asor Rosa makes an eclectic choice by establishing as basic to any literary structure the three elements of critical discourse: the text as point of departure and arrival, the literary 'system', and the relation between literature and history. "*Una buona teoria della letteratura serve a spiegare le cose come sono, mai perche' sono come sono.*" A good theory of literature serves to explain things as they are, never why they are as they are.[5]

The confusion of the 70s is caused perhaps by the fact that the cultural and political avantgard movement of the 60s was not followed by restoration but by a prolonged agony of hope of the avantgard itself. The youth of the 60s who had ridiculed literature now turns to it in a normal way.

The most organic formulation of literature and Marxist ideology is found in *Quaderni di critica* whose seven collaborators reaffirm in redefining realism, the superstructural character of art and literature.

## A PROFILE OF AN AUTHOR: LEONARDO SCIASCIA (1921-1989)

I hesitated for a while in the choice of a contemporary writer, who, in my own view and within the context of the first section of this essay — the use of the *Comedia* and the *Furioso* in a theoretical approach to the theme — best represents a successful coexistence of what I have defined for the *Comedia* as the universal and the particular.

I hesitated between Calvino and Sciascia. In considering Calvino, I was influenced by a long beautiful evening my husband Ray, a mathematician, and I spent at the home of Italo Calvino in Rome, shortly before his sudden death, to prepare for a course he had agreed to give at Columbia on Ariosto, after his lectures at Harvard. Ray and Italo were both deep in "mathematical speculations", not, however, in the abstract. The human and personal were predominant. Calvino was interested in learning more about education in America, the relation of science to literature; Ray in how a mathematician could write stories. (He was rewriting

*Genesis* in four letter words.) Both Italo and Ray were masters in the use of irony. Calvino was fascinated by the fable. They both knew the limits of reason.

I shall try to explain why my choice fell on Leonardo Sciascia. Because I never met him, I can freely imagine him in his native Sicily, in the Agrigento I so much love, writing his first story on the benches of the school where he was teaching. Perhaps he leads me back to Pirandello whose plays I directed and acted at Columbia under the guidance of Martha Abba in the early 50s.

What attracts me to Sciascia is the marvelous combination of cold irony and warm passion, the harmonious coexistence of reason and non-reason, the passion with which he embraces an idea, lives with it, working around it in his own mind until he finally translates it into most concise writing. He was extremely proud of his conciseness. He prided himself for having invented a new literary genre, the genre of the short essay.

His life stretches through Fascism, the war, the postwar moment of ecstasy, when writers believed they could write as the Voice of the People. He takes part in the intense literary debates of the avantgard in the 60s, at a distance, from the advantage point of his insular balcony, and dives ferociously into the accusation of political power in the 70s and the 80s, up to his death.

Sciascia begins very humbly by publishing a story via Calvino in "*Nuovi Argomenti,*" and publishes in 1956 and 1958 two books: *Le parrocchie di Regalpetra* and *Gli zii di Sicilia*. His great trilogy which emerged between 1961 and 1966: *Il giorno della civetta, Il Consiglio d'Egitto, A ciascuno il suo*, shows the author overwhelmed by the immensity of evil in society. Other works follow rapidly, one after the other: in 1971 *Il contesto*, a detective story immersed in contemporary politics; in 1974 *Todo Modo* another detective story or "*giallo mafioso*" (*tutti possono essere uccisi in qualsiasi momento*); for the theater *L'onorevole, I mafiosi, Commedia siciliana*. His tendency to read history in the light of contemporary events is evident. In 1975 with *La scomparsa di Majorana* he faces the problem of the scientist's responsibility versus his discoveries. A fundamental revelation of his personality is found in his 1977 *Candido, ovvero un sogno fatto in Sicilia*, where Catholicism and Communism are equally condemned. "*E se l'insieme di tante verità,*" he writes, "*fosse una grande menzogna?*" Voltaire is his idol. From this moment on, he specializes in short pieces or *Cronachette*, dealing mostly with Sicily, such as the Pirandellian *Il teatro della memoria* and the *Bruneri/Canella case*; in 1986 *La strega e il capitano*, a trial for witchery. In 1970 a collection of his writings appears, called *La corda pazza*, whose subject is Sicily, from the Arab and Norman times to the contemporary.

In 1978 *L'Affare Moro*, written a few months after the tragedy, allows Sciascia a political and linguistic analysis of Moro's letters written from prison, on the basis of which he pronounces the most ferocious condemnation of the state as it coexists with the Sicilian Mafia: "*da piu di un secolo lo stato Italiano convive con la Mafia siciliana, con la camorra napoletana e il banditismo sardo. . . . Ma ora si leva, di fronte a Moro prigioniero delle Brigate Rosse, forte e solenne. . . .*" This very same State dares to declare today that the Moro of the letters from prison is a different person from the once political man! "*Moro e'un altro*". In conclusion, Sciascia condemns the Christian Democratic Party of Moro as well as 'the others'. His aversion for the Comunist party is relentless, unconditional, categorical.

In 1979 *Nero su nero* collects various essays which focus on Sicily, but seen from the point of view of 'an Italian writer'.

Sciascia's books, through their brevity, give form to a magical mystery made of violent passion and ironic detachment. A touch of Dante and Ariosto are humbly compressed in his '*volumetto*'. He makes of a detective novel a work of art.

Neither his pessimistic view of human life, nor his violent rejection of the power of the state can kill within him a joy of living which expresses itself through writing as well as reading. He loves to deal with the present by reliving a moment of the past. His sense of the past is so genuine that it allows him to build through it a poetic Myth of the present. Not even reason can check Sciascia's poetic inspiration. He loves reason but as a poet.

> *Tu sei ben piu' rigorosamente illuminista di me — Italo Calvino wrote to him on Oct. 26, 1964 — le tue opere hanno un carattere di battaglia civile che le mie non hanno mai avuto, hanno una loro univocita' sul piano del pamphlet, anche*

*se sul piano della favola come ogni opera di poesia non possono essere ridotte ad un solo tipo di lettura* (quoted by Gianfranco Dioguardi in *Ricordo di Leonardo Sciascia* [Milano, 1993], p. 41).

You are a far more demanding Illuminist than I — your work has a sense of civil struggle that mine never did, it speaks with the unambiguous strength of the pamphlet, and yet on the level of the myth, as with all true poetry, your work cannot be reduced to a single interpretation.

I love Sciascia for the way he reads as well as for the way he writes :

*Un libro . . . e' come riscritto in ogni epoca in cui lo si legge e ogni volta che lo si legge. . . .*" (ibidem p. 40)

A book . . . is rewritten in each age in which it is read and each time it is read.

Sciascia attracts me in particular for the joy he experiences in rereading:

*E sarebbe allora il rileggere un leggere inconsapevolmente carico di tutto che tra una lettura e l'altra e' passato su quel libro e attraverso quel libro nella storia umana e dentro di noi. Ed e' percio' che la gioia del rileggere e' piu grande di quella del leggere. E si potrebbe arrivare a formulare un paradosso: che a rileggere per tutta una vita lo stesso libro si conseguirebbe maggiore felicita' che a leggere un'intera biblioteca. Naturalmente bisogna trovare un libro per cui valga la pena che tutta una vita ruoti a rileggerlo come la terra intorno al sole.* (from *Cruciverba* quoted by Dioguardi).

> And so, re-reading is itself a reading unconsciously charged with all that has taken place in the interval between the readings: to the book and, through the book, to mankind and, ultimately, to us. That is why re-reading gives us far more pleasure than reading. It constitutes something of a paradox: to read just one book for one's entire life would give greater pleasure than reading a whole library full of books. Naturally, one would have to find that particular book worth revolving a life around, as the earth around the sun.

I know now why I chose Sciascia as my favorite Italian writer among his contemporaries. As a writer, he identifies with the society about which he writes. He is at the same time a writer I can accept as a soul friend, beyond the boundaries of a given society. Because of Sciascia, I regard and study Sicily today as the microcosm of the world in which I live. Among all Italian writers he has provided me with a point not of literary, but of human reference.

## NOTES

1. The philosopher Ernesto Grassi and I made this particular myth the object of a close study within a theory of "Folly as Creativeness," a course given at Barnard and Columbia in 1984. See *Folly and Insanity in Renaissance Literature* (Binghamton, NY: MRTS, 1986), pp. 90-4, 104-06.

2. The relation of Valla's '*voluptas*' to the concept of '*follia*' and '*insania*' in the two Ferrarese poems was the subject of the course Grassi and I offered at Columbia in 1983 (see note above). As for Valla's dialogue "On Pleasure," see M. de Panizza Lorch, *A Defense of Life. Lorenzo Valla's Theory of Pleasure* (Munchen: Fink Verlag, 1985); L. Valla, *De Vero Falsoque Bono*, critical ed. by Maristella de Panizza Lorch (Bari: Adriatica, 1970); Lorenzo Valla, *On Pleasure/De voluptate*, trans. by Kent Hieatt and Maristella Lorch, Intro. by Lorch (Abaris Books, 1977).

The issue has been dealt with also in specific articles.

3. Italy counterbalances our Raymond Chandler, Dashiel Hammet, Jim Thompson with Alessandro Barrico in *Oceano/mare*, Andrea Camilleri in *Il ladro di merendine*, Ferrandino in *Pericle il Nero* (a day in the life of a gangster told in the first person). Publishing houses like New Directions and Steer Force, as well as translators like Bill Weaver, have given the Italian *noir* particular attention.)

4. Again in this case, I find in my own library a generous competent Virgil who guides me through the thick forest of attacks and counterattacks, journals, congresses, debates and ferocious disputes. My main reference book is Petrocchi's and Giannantonio's superb *Letteratura, Cultura e Societa' del Novecento* (Naples, 1974).

It is mostly, however, Giuliano Manacorda who, first in the courses he gave at Columbia within the "Center for International Exchange" and now through his two volumes, leads me through the past forty years of Italian debates on the relation of literature to society. I treasure as great gifts his *Storia della letteratura italiana contemporanea* (1940-1975) published in Rome 1979 and his *Letteratura italiana d'oggi* 1965-1985, published in Rome in 1987.

5. Useful for the purpose is A. Berardinelli, *Trasformazione dell'idea di letteratura nel corso del decennio '70.*

## CHAPTER III

# THE ITALIAN ECONOMY FACING THE EURO-CHALLENGE

*GIANNANDREA FALCHI*

## INTRODUCTION

An examination of the first eleven months of the European Monetary Union (EMU) reveals that financial markets have encountered few problems in adapting to the Euro, and also shows that business flowing through these markets has evolved broadly in line with expectations.

The strong rise in the volume of private bond issues, for instance, has provided early validation of the view that capital markets will play an increasingly important role in meeting the funding needs of Euro zone companies.

On foreign exchange markets, the USD/Euro rate weakened as demand for the Euro was affected by the expectations of higher U.S. interest rates and by the sluggish economic performance of EMU countries.

Currency watchers are now looking for the Euro to recover in response to acceleration in Europe's real GDP growth. Indeed, several indicators point to the long awaited rebound in business activity; industrial production indicators have turned around, there has been a correction in inventories and orders are rising. In this context, the rate of growth of the Italian economy is expected to double from 1.4 percent this year to 2.7 percent next year.

The purpose of this lecture is to analyze the Italian economic and financial system and to evaluate the structural problems that still affect it. Only by solving these problems, in fact, will Italy be able to fully seize the opportunities made available by participation in the EMU and be part of the recovery of the European economy.

## THE ITALIAN ECONOMY

### *Growth*

During the 1990s the United States registered an economic growth characterized by low unemployment and inflation rates. Fixed investments in the United States grew at an annual average of 5.8 percent, raising the ratio of investments to GDP from 13 to 17 percent. One third of total investments were recorded in the manufacturing industry. The same amount was spent in computer goods. In the same period, capital stock per employee did not increase significantly, despite the high trend of investment, due to a 1.8 percent annual average of employment growth.

In the last eight years, the European Union has adopted economic policies aimed at containing public deficits in an unfavorable economic cycle. Average annual growth in fixed investments was 0.6 percent, 40 percent of which was in manufacturing. Although capital stock per employee was boosted by a high rate of unemployment, it has remained lower than that of the United States. Furthermore, during the same period, the number of employed persons in Italy declined.

An uncertain growth perspective, coupled with an ageing population (18 percent of the Italian population is composed of persons over the age of 65), has diminished the tendency to invest. In Italy, limited job opportunities and high fiscal pressures are reflected in a low percentage of the population active in the job force (60 percent, compared to 68 percent in the United States).

Moreover, the industrial sector is characterized by a middle technology, which faces competition with the less stringent regulations and low labor and tax costs of emerging countries. The fiscal burden in Italy is high in contrast, if one considers both the income taxes and the social contributions paid by businesses and workers.

Future measures should include: an increase in the quality of services, fiscal policies aimed at expanding potential growth, improved efficiency in public administration and a relaxation of business regulations.

## *Labor Market*

In Italy, there are a few bottlenecks in the labor market, which still impede the proper allocation of human resources. Employment growth requires greater flexibility both in legislation and work contracts.

During the most recent period, a higher number of temporary jobs were filled. A greater increase in turnover took place in industrial firms, while temporary jobs of more than six months became commonplace in major companies. This latter job category reached 9 percent of total jobs, compared to 13 percent in the European Union. Part-time workers make up 7 percent of the workforce.

In light of the higher rate of per-capita working hours in respect to past years, more flexible contractual agreements have allowed for an increase in the number of persons employed and a reduction in irregular working conditions. One may observe the tendency towards a decrease of full-time long term workers, in favor of those with less stable contracts.

A high level of self-employment and small businesses characterize employment in Italy.

Self-employed persons, with the exclusion of those in farming, are particularly numerous in commerce, making up more than 25 percent of the workforce, almost double the European average. Businesses employing fewer than 10 workers represent about 90 percent of all Italian businesses, and employ 45 percent of all workers. Large businesses, with more than 250 employees, employ 20 percent of the workforce.

Smaller businesses reflect high and innovative levels of professionalism, allowing for the indirect utilization of more flexible and less costly services. These companies have increased the economy's ability to deal with sharp market fluctuations. During the last 20 years, they have been able to curb unemployment in the manufacturing industry and have contributed to roughly half of all Italian sales abroad.

However, in the future, labor policies cannot overlook the phenomenon of market globalization, which has favored the expansion of international trade. For this reason, in more developed countries, and particularly in Italy, economic activity has shifted towards the service industry, in some cases making up 70 percent of GDP. Nevertheless, efficiency in these sectors can be attained only through advanced technology and high levels of skill.

Competition is also developing in the areas of medium and high technology. It is necessary for Italy to move toward higher added value sectors and to increase economic efficiency by developing a more flexible labor market.

Italy is working toward the reform of employment rights and industrial relations. This should help to limit social and economic costs, consisting in many cases of the unemployment of the younger workforce members.

Workers should also benefit more directly in company profits, allowing wages to move in line with the evolution of a firm's economic situation, as determined by structural changes, cyclical fluctuations, or variations in output.

Productivity is still low in areas with a high youth unemployment rate, because of insufficient investment in public infrastructures. In these areas, there is evidence of social problems, which curb the creation of small and medium-sized businesses. Labor costs in these regions are still high and, in some cases, equilibrium wages are lower than official wages.

The participation rate of the Italian labor force is lower than that prevailing in other developed countries. A large segment of the population is discouraged from participating in the labor market by low expectations of finding a job. Together with a high percentage of underground employment, this indicates a poor connection between labor supply conditions and labor productivity.

Laws and institutions must create ideal conditions for raising the participation rate and easing long-term and youth unemployment. Some steps in this direction have been taken thanks to the introduction of more flexible working conditions which, so far, have had positive results. Public effort, as required by social interest, is limited by the weight of public debt.

### *Budget Deficit*

The role of the public sector and the size and structure of the budget are fundamental in establishing guidelines for the development of the Italian economy in the coming years.

Efforts to reduce the budget deficit, initiated with determination in the early 90s, were intensified with the approach of the single currency deadline. Public sector deficit has declined from 9.2 percent of GDP in 1994 to 2.8 percent in 1998; it should be around 2.0 percent this year.

This adjustment was based on an increase in revenue: the ratio of taxes and social security contributions to GDP rose from 39 percent to 44 percent from 1990 to 1998.

Expenditure, excluding interest payments, declined from 46 percent of GDP in 1993 to 42 percent this year.

Pension reforms, combined with cuts in transfers to non-state public bodies, have prevented primary current expenditure from rising faster than GDP in recent years. Public sector wages and salaries have been held in check by income policies and restrictions in recruitment.

The rapid ageing of the population, however, will cause spending on pensions to rise in relation to GDP. The ratio of the population aged 65 and over, to that aged between 15 and 64, has doubled since the beginning of the 60s and now stands at 25 percent.

Action must be taken to forestall the difficulties that will otherwise arise in the coming years. It is necessary to act promptly to reduce pension benefits in relation to GDP. Workers will be able to obtain the coverage they desire by taking out supplementary pensions.

The ageing population also increases the demand for health and welfare services. In the medium term, keeping expenditures within the limits compatible with the growth of national income and the supply of adequate services will require a socially acceptable revision of the right to access benefits. Supplementary private insurance can make a contribution.

## THE ITALIAN BANKING AND FINANCIAL SYSTEM

### *Stock Market*

While the Italian banking and financial system has become more integrated in the global economy, there is still a gap compared to other industrialized countries. The ratio of gross financial assets to GDP in 1985 was 5.7 in the United States, 6.4 in Japan and 7.6 in the United Kingdom, and increased greatly in the following years. The average in the four major Euro countries was 4.5 in 1985 and 6.8 in 1998; in Italy it was 5.5 in 1998.

The expansion of the stock market is limited by the low propensity of medium to large sized businesses to become listed and by the great number of small businesses that do not resort to the market. The value of stock exchange capitalization is 52 percent of GDP. German capitalization accounts for 55 percent of GDP, Spanish and French for 75 percent and 80 percent respectively. In the United States the ratio is near 180 percent.

There are currently 240 listed companies, slightly above the number in 1994. During this period in Germany, national listed companies went from 420 to 750, in France from 490 to 760 and in the United Kingdom from 2,070 to 2,400.

Compared to 1994, stock market transactions have gone up, from 60 percent to 100 percent of capitalization. Derivatives trading has grown substantially, with positive effects on the underlying markets.

The limited size of the stock market reflects the peculiar productive structure of Italy, dominated by small businesses. The main deterrents of market quotation are the fear of losing company control and the greater costs related to higher visibility.

A general reform of corporate law for the promotion of growth and competition in domestic businesses is under way. The goal of the reform is the simplification of regulations, the widening of statutory autonomy, and the valorization of the entrepreneurial nature of business, while respecting transparency. Such reform would keep managerial and organizational costs of small and medium sized businesses from rising.

During the last few years, due to the large amounts of liquidity in the international markets and interest rate differentials, there has been a strong increase of foreign investment in Italian bonds. Investments reached 125,000 billion lire in 1996 and remained at similar levels in 1997, while they arrived at 192,000 billion in 1998.

In the first nine months of 1999 there were net purchases of foreign securities by residents, due to a decline in the yields of Italian public bonds, and to the tendency of Italian investors to diversify their portfolios. Italian portfolio investments abroad were equal to 179,000 billion lire, while foreign investments in Italy amounted to 133,000 billion lire.

Foreign direct investments by Italian companies are also rising: from 9,000 billion lire in 1996 to 17,500 billion in 1997 and 22,000 billion in 1998. Inversely, foreign direct investments in Italy were 4,500 billion lire in 1998, lower than those made in previous years. By the end of 1998, the stock of direct investments abroad held by Italian companies was 273,000 billion lire against investments in Italy by non-residents of 174,000 billion.

In the first nine months of this year Italian companies made 109 acquisitions abroad, up 22 percent with respect to the same period in 1998 and almost 50 percent compared to 1996.

Domestic companies are capable of diversification and show interest in markets where production costs are lower and the prospects of sales seem favorable. Nevertheless, there is a partial delocalization of productive activity, even towards economically advanced systems.

The ability to attract investors must be reinforced. Differences in cost and taxation still exist in comparison to other European countries. Progress must be made in reducing the complexity of business regulations and in improving the low efficiency of public administration.

*Banking System*

Banca d'Italia has raised the degree of competition in the banking system substantially in the last few years. Following the adoption of European directives, many operative restrictions were lifted. Supervisory activity has turned from structural to prudential, and aims at verifying capital ratio adequacy, while maintaining the directors' autonomy in the allocation of resources. The "*Testo Unico*" of 1993 abolished the separation between commercial and investment banks.

Competition and product innovation were also fueled by the presence of numerous foreign intermediaries. The market share of foreign bank branches went up, in terms of assets, from 3 percent to 7 percent during the 1990s. The presence of foreign intermediaries is particularly strong in the sectors of consumer lending, government bond trading and corporate finance.

Foreign banks also have relevant holdings in a number of Italian credit institutions. Today, French, German, Spanish and Dutch banks are significant shareholders of the major Italian banks. Foreign capital represents more that 10 percent of the capital of each of the first five banking groups.

Increased competition can be observed in the higher number of banks per province, up from 24 in 1985 to 31 and in the reduction of the spread between lending and deposit rates.

To reach the level of efficiency required by higher competition, more decisional freedom was given to administrative boards, allowing them to confront problems related to cost reduction and the innovation of products.

The increased autonomy of boards occurred in two phases. In the first stage, public institutions were given incentives to become incorporated, as this would create more favorable conditions for economically positive results and favor merger operations.

In the second stage, also thanks to this transformation, the privatization process of the system, whose assets were held mainly by the government and various local authorities, was set in motion and steadily has gained pace. As a result, the amount of assets owned by the government and local authorities fell from 68 percent in 1992 to the current 12 percent.

*Consolidation*

The EMU has influenced the ownership control and size of credit institutions. The creation of a European market, in which price dynamics are more transparent and not conditioned by exchange rate fluctuations, has encouraged households and businesses to make more efficient decisions in regards to consumption and investments. On the one hand, banks have acquired new potential clients, on the other, they are subject to more competition.

Faced with the need to reduce costs and to assume more competitive organizational and dimensional structures, along with privatization, a process of consolidation is underway. During the last few years the process has involved more than 450 banks, and has accounted for 40 percent of total assets.

The number of banks has fallen from 1,156 in 1990 to 876 at present. The first five banking groups hold some 50 percent of total assets (up from 35 percent only three years ago), a value in line with those of the major European partners. Yet, the Italian banking system still appears of less significant dimensions within Europe. The first five Italian banking groups account for 6 percent of the total assets of the European banking system, compared to 13, 12 and 10 percent held, respectively, by the leading banking groups of Germany, France and the United Kingdom.

Banca d'Italia plays a major role in the merger process. Italian consolidation regulations, based on European directives, ensure the sound and prudent management and the integrity of the banking system. As in major financial systems, it is required that any significant acquisition of banking capital first be examined and authorized by the supervisory authorities.

The consolidation process is not meant to impede the coexistence of small and medium sized banks with large ones. The former should provide services to local economies, the latter should have a greater interest in global markets.

*Competition*

The increase of competition in the intermediation of deposits requires a higher quality of service at a competitive cost. In the last two years, advances have been made in the management of household savings. ATM machines have become numerous, as branches and other technological advances in customer service have increased.

There is room for Italian banks to obtain significant results in the area of corporate finance. A recent bill on securitization could give this sector a boost.

Compared to a peak in 1993, the number of employees has declined by 8 percent, bringing the industry's workforce to 311,000 units. The number of employees per branch, which is quite low by international standards, has declined.

This reduction was realized by means of mergers and restructuring programs, mostly in the form of early retirement packages offered to a large number of near-retirement employees. Costs per employee were 118.4 million lire in 1997 and fell to

114.5 million in 1999.

The higher level of competition reached by the Italian banking system has lowered the cost of services and stimulated innovation. Nevertheless, in order to achieve a return on equity aligned with that of the other major banking systems, the cost of labor per product unit must decrease, while revenues from services need to be higher.

In this context, an agreement between banking associations and trade unions has been passed, with the objective of bringing costs nearer to European levels and obtaining a closer correlation between the cost per employee and the profitability of each bank.

## CONCLUSION

For most of this decade Italy has advanced, driven by two external forces: Europe and the markets. Political pressure was brought on by the deadlines and conditions of the Monetary Union, together with economic pressure consisting of the international financial markets' continuous judgment of Italy's ability to meet EMU membership criteria.

Since the beginning of the year, a new phase has begun with an easing of both pressures. Italy faces new challenges today: to generate the same kind of catalyst which permitted its entry in the Euro and to solve the structural problems that still affect it.

The Italian economy must return to a faster pace of growth. This can be attained, thanks to its resources, not only in savings, but also in technical and managerial expertise.

A stronger growth rate will contribute substantially to the balancing of public accounts. In order to boost employment, there is need for greater flexibility in utilizing the factors of production and a tighter correlation between wages, on one side, and productivity and company performance, on the other. An increase in employment resulting from flexibility alone would ultimately increase the precariousness of labor relations.

The opportunities made available by EMU participation should be fully seized upon with an economic policy that creates an environment suitable for profitable investments and company growth, and which eliminates those regulatory, fiscal and financial factors that still hinder entrepreneurial activity.

## CHAPTER IV

# WUI: WRITING UNDER THE INFLUENCE: Journalism and Power in Post-War Italy

*VITTORIO ZUCCONI*

Journalism is one of those professions that have elicited more cheap jokes and one-liners by comedians and authors than can be quoted in a single conversation. We are probably only surpassed by dentists, lawyers, used-car sales persons, stockbrokers and politicians as objects of contempt and resentment by the public. This is not a joke: studies and polls, conducted in the United States as well as in Europe, consistently show that newspeople, including pundits, reporters, commentators and anchors, are considered to be the lowest tier by people. We are seen as self-aggrandizing, embellishing, lying, phony, blow-dried, up-for-sale slobs with an agenda (usually a liberal and/or a leftist one) — and I am sparing you the really bad names.

The great British writer, G.K. Chesterton, who tried his hand at defining what journalism is, came up with this line: "Journalism is a profession for lazy people who are ashamed of themselves, but who are not ashamed enough to get a real job". Perhaps this is the reason why journalism in all its forms has never been a more popular and sought after profession than it is now. Journalism majors are springing up everywhere. Even in Italy, where journalism was not considered a subject worthy of scholarly attention, every major university is now offering post-graduate degrees in journalism, more often than not taught by journalists who never received a B.A. themselves.

Having taught a few classes in Italian colleges, I have often wondered why it is that in Italy journalism has always been regarded in academia as a post-grad, advanced level degree, open only to mature students. Perhaps because young, immature men and women should not be exposed to harmful substances like alcohol, tobacco, mutual funds and journalism at an early, impressionable age.

If I come across to you as slightly cynical and jaded towards my chosen profession — and chosen it was, to the great despair of my father who was a professional journalist himself for 50 years and thus had higher hopes for his firstborn son — it is because I have been at this job for thirty-five years. Working in Italy for various Italian media, I was deprived of any illusions at a very young age.

I started out when only nineteen. I had just finished high school, and was about to go to college in Milan in an attempt to become a clinical psychologist. My mother was — with good motive — worried that I was a good-for-nothing child of the '60s, so she pestered me to "at least get a job" while pretending to attend classes. I did. I became an intern at a small paper, where I covered the crime beat and city hall. I dropped psychology and turned to modern history. When I got to my thesis, it took me a long while to finish it, and my professor, a very demanding and stern historian by the name of Marino Berengo, gave me an almost unheard of summa cum laude degree. This, of course, greatly surprised me, my parents, and especially my more diligent friends who were working much harder just to get by.

After the ceremony, the handshaking, and all the formal things that occur when a degree is bestowed upon one in Europe, the professor approached me and said, in his earnest, stern, serious way:

> You wrote a massive thesis on Europe after Metternich and the Vienna Congress of 1815 (the same subject dear to Henry Kissinger, I would discover later, but all analogies must end there). I did not believe a single word that you wrote. The research was amateurish, your imagination took over, and you don't know the first thing about being a true historian. But as the head of the History Department' — he added with a half smile, a full half more than his usual forbidding expression - 'I have to read dozens of theses every year, and I never enjoyed reading one as much as I did yours. It was not history, of course, but it was great. Even we college professors get bored, you know, and we like to read something pleasurable once in a

while, so thank you very much for your work.

That was as perfect a definition of the First Commandment of journalism as there could be: Thou shall be read or get out and get a real job. At that moment my future as a journalist was cast.

But what is it then to be a journalist in Italy, if you go beyond the First Commandment? Is it to be a readable "amateur historian" as I was in college? Is it "fun," as so many of our young generation think, judging by the growing number of those who try their hand at it? Is it financially profitable? Is it glamorous and exciting, now that television has made stars of once humble and deservedly obscure hacks? Or is it a higher calling to be, as it should, the guard dog of free speech, truth and news, constantly nibbling at the heels of the powerful and deceitful?

Some of the above, certainly, and yet none of the above. My dear professor's off-handed compliments notwithstanding, being a journalist in Italy has been and is still a hard, frustrating, and at times depressing and exasperating profession that every day, through every word and every piece we write, brings us all in touch with the hard face of our unforgiving history.

## NEWSPAPERS

Like all other forms of cultural and political expression in our history, journalism has always been a "top-down" exercise, where few but often well-meaning intellectuals rain their opinions "down" onto the populace. Very rare are the examples of publications that travel the opposite route, from "the bottom" of the civil and religious pyramid up, in the Anglo tradition of small local newspapers. In one word, journalism — as well as religion, political and economic power — has traditionally been reserved for the elite. As well-intentioned as some of the elite might have been, the news business has always been a secondary expression of primary interests. In one word the press in Italy has tended throughout history to play an ancillary role; not the "Fourth Power", but the arm of some other power.

One of Italy's most famous and respected journalists, Mario Missiroli, for a whole generation editor of the leading daily, Milan's *Corriere della Sera*, used to sigh when his reporters complained about the timidity of his editorial choices: "I know; . . . I know . . . if I only had a newspaper in my hand, the things I could write." He was not kidding.

He was simply expressing the frustration of feeling, with our own fingers and our own words, the frailty of our relatively young and struggling democracy, the maddening "crazy quilt" of compromise, inbreeding and plain complicity that was and has always been Italy's politics and social life.

A reporter, a commentator, or a managing editor are objectively soldiers in the front line trenches of democracy. No one feels the impact of all the traditions and history that have impeded the full development of a truly independent press in our country more directly. Freedom of the press is distributed, conceded, and allocated, but almost never, if ever, conquered from below. And this is the exact opposite definition of what a free press should be. Not something *octroye*, as the French say, not something conceded from above, but something conquered from below.

No one, for better or for worse, has ever thrown tea overboard in Italy, nor stormed a Winter Palace. No violent revolution nor insurrection has ever succeeded in Italy, albeit many have been started. Italy is the land of "*revolutio interrupta*". Compromise and intrigue have been the grist for the Italian political mill since good Brutus felt, and rightly so, that Caesar was leaning dangerously toward too much personal power and "personality cult". As a reward for his efforts, Republican Rome became an Empire. Revolutions just do not work in Italy.

You will not be shocked if I tell you that we are all children of the past. We are all the products of our own history. This is true even of Americans, who grow up believing that history is a subject for TV trivia games and everything relevant starts tomorrow. History is what makes us who we are. And of course journalism does not exist without history. Journalism is the fish, big or small, pretty or ugly, who swims in the society in which it is practiced and could not exist in the abstract. It can be worse than the society in which it swims, but it certainly cannot be much better than the culture that nourishes and/or starves it .

In essence, to be a journalist in Italy and to some extent in Europe is thus to swim against the current of a tradition that has never seen the kind of unabridged freedom and independence enjoyed — I should say, taken for granted — in the United States. When journalism is bad, as it so often is now in the United States, newspeople have nobody to blame but themselves. We in Italy, at least, have a few little alibis to hide behind when we are bad.

There is no Second Amendment in Italy, as there is no *habeas corpus* in the Roman jurisprudence tradition, or even in the French Napoleonic Code that was imposed upon us some centuries ago by Bonaparte's bayonets. Freedom of the press in Italy does not need to be protected. It has to be yanked and finessed — piece by piece, day after day, line after line — from the hands of the powerful, whoever the powerful are, in a constant battle of ground conquered and ground lost. And we don't have to look back at the Julius Caesars, Kings or Popes to see where the roots of this "unfreedom" of the media reside. Even history as recent as 50 years ago reinforced the long held belief that freedom of the press has to be tempered and tamed.

My professional life coincides with most of the post-war period of the Italian new-found democracy. I remember that as a young man I was enthused, excited and inspired to become a reporter by reading a great little newspaper that was published in Milan, called *Il Giorno*, "The Day". It came out in the early 60s and was written by a group of great, open-minded, aggressive journalists, who produced a publication that was unlike any other of its time. That publication was the perfect example of the problems that we, as newspeople, had to face and are still facing in Italy.

The young men and — a rarity — the young women who made *Il Giorno,* thought of themselves as a new breed of writers, the post-Fascist generation. Their product was irreverent, well-written, investigative and factual. In short, it was what a daily paper should be and never before had been in Italy. It enjoyed great success until overnight, this great newspaper withered because it was owned and financed by an Italian industrial giant called ENI, the national oil company, and by the man who chaired this organization, Enrico Mattei.

As long as Mattei was alive, and as long as he wanted to have an aggressive, independent, "pain-in-the-neck-of-the-government" publication to further his main interest, the oil business, this paper flourished, and Italian reporters showed that they could be as inquisitive and courageous as all the Woodward and Bernsteins of this world.

But as soon as he died, in a very dubious and, to this day, still unexplained private plane crash, and the company was taken over and "normalized" by some faceless bureaucrats in the Italian government, this newspaper wilted away. The magnificent men and women who made that paper, *Il Giorno*, found out that they had been *allowed* to be aggressive and independent. They had never been truly independent. They were writing under the influence. It was a benign and positive influence, but an influence nonetheless.

The influences that we write under originate, to be fair, both from within and from without. And none of them is more insidious and pervasive than the deeply rooted Italian conviction that power is dangerous, must be tamed, courted and, most of all, shared. It is not by chance, but by design, that Italy is the land of political revolving doors, of "musical chairs" governments, and of innumerable parties whose sole purpose is not to conquer power, but to carve a slice of power.

Foreign observers often smile at the "instability" of Italian politics, without realizing that Italy — with Japan — has been by far the most politically stable nation of the so-called industrialized world. The constant turnover of Prime Ministers and cabinet members was nothing but window dressing to blur the reality of the same old groups and faces perpetually in power, power being, of course, a relative expression, because in Italy no one has had real political power in the latter part of the 20th Century.

Centuries of mostly bad experiences with local tyrants, kings, foreign warlords and Popes have ingrained in the DNA of generations of Italians that the best you can expect from a ruler is the least harm he can do. Therefore, the equation is simple: never give anyone enough power to do damage. There could be a Mussolini lurking behind that bespectacled, harmless looking *professore* if he or she (sadly, I'm just being politically correct here, because there is no history of a "she" in power besides Lucrezia Borgia in Italy) is given enough power. Why take the chance? Why allow those pesky, "irresponsible" journalists to upset the apple cart with their words? Was not Mussolini a journalist? He was, and a very good one, I'm afraid to admit.

*The Bounds of Freedom*

The immediate post-World War II period, in all its apparent new found "freedom", did nothing to change the minimalist, prudent, and pessimist outlook that matured through generations and was thrust upon the shoulders of journalists whose first duty was considered to be helping maintain the *status quo*. On the contrary, the Cold War locked the media in frozen, opposing camps of "pro-Western" and "pro-Eastern" players who were — as in an opera theater — called upon to sing a pre-written libretto of "bad guys" and "good guys".

The Fascists' explicit oppression of free speech was replaced by a tacit, but iron clad, post-war covenant of complicity, forged in the harsh transition between Fascism and the Cold War. The hard oppression of dictatorship in Italy was replaced by the "soft tyranny" of consensus, forced upon us by the presence of the largest Communist party in the non-Communist world.

Italy found itself on the verge of going from the hot stove of Il Duce to the frying pan of Yosif Stalin. It was thus a given, in 1947 and 1948, that if the Communists had won the elections, Italy would have fallen under the influence of the Soviet Bloc, becoming at best a sunnier and better-tempered Yugoslavia. Therefore, we in the press were taught, directly and indirectly by our elders, that our first duty was to not rock the boat, because, had the boat been rocked, we might have all fallen into the hands of Moscow, and the Cossacks — as the propaganda of the day literally went — would have "watered their horses at the fountains in St. Peter's Square."

Whatever freedom of the press we grabbed, it then had to be measured against this immense responsibility, real or perceived. Is a story, a scandal, a scalding editorial, an investigative report — we were asked — worth helping the Cossacks' horses drink the Holy Water of St. Peter by favoring the "Opposition", the Reds? Of course not. The fate of 50 million Italians was in our hands, we were told. We were free to do and write whatever we wanted, under the new laws and the new Constitution. But the paradox before us was subtle and cruel: if we exercised in full our new found freedom and attacked the government, we would have "played into the hands of the Communists," and in the end, would have destroyed the very liberty that we were exercising.

As the whole country was forced into a pigeonhole during the dangerous game of Eastern versus Western ideological confrontation, so was the Media.

Even as we emerged from Fascism, freedom of the press was immediately under somebody's control. Who? the Allied Powers who were occupying Italy. You could not print newspapers in 1946-47 in Italy without having paper to print with, and who controlled paper? the U.S. generals, the administrators for the occupying force. Once again, we had to beg somebody for our freedom to be free and to print, and that reinforced a mental attitude of dependence.

If you criticized or opposed the government, you were immediately labeled a communist, because there was no true opposition other than the Communists. Every young, aspiring reporter, as well as seasoned journalists, had to choose. Either we were in, or we were out of the assigned pigeonhole. Newspapers had to tow the line, not necessarily the party line, but the great dividing line between democracy and non-democracy, freedom and non-freedom, the East and the West. We lived on the border line between two worlds, we were the "soft underbelly of NATO", in the patronizing idiom of the Cold War, and we were the armies fighting in the trenches between the two. Fighting in the trenches is notoriously not conducive to freedom of expression.

The press was free to choose sides, and this was certainly huge progress compared to Fascist times. But it was not yet "the freedom to be free". It was more the equivalent of "any color you want, as long as it is black", as Henry Ford would have put it. One could be a Communist, if one so chose, or a Right Winger, or a Christian Centrist or a Social Democrat, but once the costume of the chosen part was donned, one had to follow the game plan. No free-lancing was allowed. Again, as in the opera theater, one had to play one's part and sing one's songs, according to the music.

Naturally, the singers, the actors and the choir have to be well-paid and well-treated in order for them to sing and act in tune. They all had to be kept happy and well-fed, and members of the Media were, as individuals and as an industry.

Every person and every party, as miniscule as they might be, would have to be given their own little gardens to cultivate.

The money- the public money- was generously given by the ever-ruling majority, as well as the tools and the time to tend each plot in the great Media Garden. And an extraordinary, uniquely Italian media phenomenon was born: the atrocious "party paper". Dozens of "party newspapers" were born and printed, all lavishly financed by the public Treasury, regardless of their quality or even their circulation, which was always very modest. The one exception was the Communists' "official organ", *L'Unità,* which was dutifully bought as an act of faith by the party loyalists. No matter how small the Party and how insignificant its audience or its constituency, every political formation had a God-given right to print a rag and feed a good number of its followers, posing as journalism.

It was the opposite of real journalism and a distorted "training center" for generations of young reporters who were hired and forever ruined in newsrooms whose sole purpose was to push the party line. So ingrained was this practice — reproduced as we will see in the larger world of broadcasting — that many of my Italian colleagues were incredulous when I tried to explain to them that in the United States the two major parties do not have their own papers, at least not overtly. If marginal parties that barely got one per cent of the general vote had full fledged dailies, often with foreign offices, correspondents, columnist, sport pages, how could the Grand Old Party or the Party of FDR and JFK not have a newspaper, they asked.

To this day, when old walls are supposed to have crumbled, publishers receive huge amounts of public money, in the apparent, noble goal of "sustaining a free and diverse press". The object of the game is obviously much less lofty: it is to keep the media industry somehow "endentured" and dependent. Many papers would not survive an hour longer if the State's subisidies were to be withdrawn. The habit of dependency — and therefore complicity — is hard to kick. Recently, an historic masthead in Italy's history went under, the old Communist paper *l'Unità,* for lack of circulation. Not even the State's subsidy could keep afloat a daily paper that went from a million copies sold to 50,000 per day, and that was a perverse and painful demonstration that perhaps things are beginning to change for the better.

But for decades it was, to belabor my point, Italian Opera, or Operetta Buffa, a mere representation of media freedom and free market. Party papers, no matter how numerous they are, do not a free press make, and the sum of many different lies does not a truth make. Even the major dailies, Milan's *Corriere della Sera,* Turin's *La Stampa,* Rome's *Il Messaggero* and, in the late '70s, *La Repubblica* were forced to take sides in the ideological battle between East and West, and they subjected journalism to the suffocating, all-encompassing imperative of politics. If you did not take sides in the pantomime, you made everybody else uncomfortable.

I was shocked to find how crystallized this role-playing, this "representation" of a free press, had become when I went back to Italy in 1977, after having worked around the world and in the United States for about 10 years. I started reporting for the *Corriere della Sera*, Milan's newspaper, on domestic politics. I went to Rome and covered the election of our president, Sandro Pertini, a few governmental crises and major political figures. I naively wrote whatever I saw, whatever I thought, and my colleagues were taken aback.

The first question I was asked upon returning was always: 'Whose side are you on? Are you a Christian Democrat, are you a Socialist, are you a Commie, on the left, on the right, in the middle?' I said "I don't know. I'm just a journalist', and they all laughed at me and said, "He's back from America, but he thinks he still lives there'.

One day I went to cover a famous and unsinkable Italian politician by the name of Giulio Andreotti. I followed him around for a few days, from dawn to dusk. I realized that, contrary to the "lazy bum" stereotype of Italian politics, he was an indefatigable, hard worker and a true practitioner of his Catholic faith. He woke up at the crack of dawn. He went to Mass and received the Eucharist every day. He read every newspaper, every text of a proposed law, and answered every piece of correspondence personally. I wrote a story accordingly. The next day, when I went to see my colleagues - journalists travel in a pack like wolves or sheep, tending to stay together - they all looked relieved. `Now we know- they smiled - you are pro-Andreotti'. What?

I went to Turin and covered the Socialist Party Congress, led at the time by Bettino Craxi, and he gave a speech which was one of the finest political speeches I have ever heard in Italy. I wrote that he gave a great speech, and of course my friends were taken aback: 'We thought you were with Andreotti, and now you approve of Craxi? What are you, for God's sake?'. I became so angry and disenchanted that I left Italy and went back abroad to Moscow in 1979 to once again work as a foreign correspondent. At least the Russians were honest. They did not pretend to give you freedom of the press. You knew where you stood with Soviets as a journalist, and there was no pigeonholing in the old USSR; just a big old cage for all.

But the domestication of the Italian daily and electronic media in the '70 and '80, left a crack that not even the soft tyranny of consensus and the spreading of favors could close. While the newspapers were doing their job of playing their part in the opera, there was an explosion of magazines and periodicals.

Luckily, information is like water. You can try and channel and contain it as much as you want, but unless you find a way to dry it up entirely, it will find its way through the cracks. Just like that, the press found a way to satisfy the public demand for more aggressive reporting in the weekly magazines by publishing lively political and popular periodicals that did the job that the major dailies and the state-owned TV and radio networks could not, or would not do.

They dealt with lifestyle issues, sports, travel, women's issues, such as abortion, sex, divorce, corruption, and inefficiency; everything one wanted to know but could not find in the stuffy newspapers of the time. Not by chance, while the circulation of the major dailies stagnated, (Italian dailies sell globally in the year 2000 as much, or as little, as they sold in 1960), weeklies like *Espresso, Panorama, Oggi,* and *Gente,* exploded. Even today, in the year 2000, the largest circulation numbers belong to a magazine. It's a Christian magazine, and it's called *Famiglia Cristiana,* "Christian Family". It sells well over a million copies a week, which is an enormous figure by Italian standards, and it is considered one of the most objective and better balanced publications in Italy. Under the umbrella of its generic Christian label, *Famiglia Cristiana* has courageously pushed the envelope on many sensitive subjects, like sexual behavior or cheating in major professional sports, often incurring the displeasure of the Church's hierarchy.

Magazines were, in the postwar period, the "odd player out", the "court jester" in the stilted play of the mainstream Media. The ruling parties and their accomplices, the so-called opposition, did not mind them too much, in fact they liked them and cherished them, because they told some necessary truths and were basically irrelevant, read only by the "hairdresser" clientele, the patients in the doctor's waiting room and the always harmless intellectuals. What the government wanted was the effective neutrality of the major dailies and control of the airwaves, and these it had in full.

## TELEVISION

Enter RAI. RAI, the ancient and cute acronym that, since the not so roaring twenties, stands for *Radio Audizioni Italiane* was and still is the state radio and television monopoly created by Mussolini and eagerly preserved by the post-war "democratic" parties, that were only too happy to pick up where Il Duce had left off and to expand their control of the airwaves in their own manner.

### *RAI*

Under the guise of serving the "Public Interest", and being owned by the State and not by private investors, RAI became in effect and remained for decades a propaganda tool in the hands of whomever controlled the State, i.e. the ruling parties. When the first TV broadcasts began in Italy, in 1954, they were of course originated by RAI, the only entity authorized by the laws (written and approved by the ruling coalitions) to broadcast anything.

And the party, or parties, in government were not satisfied with control of the one and only TV network in Italy, thanks to laws that they themselves had passed: they also forced the citizens to pay a "yearly subscription" to enjoy the privilege of watching that channel. I still remember the first black and white TV bought by my father in 1957: it was an American-made Dumont and had only one button, on and off. No need to tune or change anything. It was pre-tuned to the only existing channel, RAI. We had no choice, and yet we had to pay for this lack of options.

It was an extraordinary arrangement, a tribute to the

diabolical genius of the politicians and the infinite patience of the Italians. The voters, the people, had to pay to watch what the government wanted them to see, in the name of a public service where the only public being serviced were the Mandarins in power.

It is a tribute to the resilience of the Italian people and the clumsiness of the TV daily pablum of non-news, that not even the Christian Democrats could avoid losing elections and being forced to forge political alliances to stay in power. Left-wing parties like the Socialists had to be enticed into the majority, to support the fading Christian Democrats, and had to be rewarded accordingly. In the time-honored tradition of Italian history, they got upgraded to modern technology and a share of the power, and in this case it was a share of the media power.

A second TV network was created in the 60s (still with public money), out of the state monopoly, to accommodate the Socialists and was graciously given to them. In Italy, we don't shoot or imprison, or even defeat opponents to vanquish them; we offer them a job. We offer their children, spouses, lovers, cousins, brothers and sisters-in-law, and friends a job. It is, of course, the classic Roman technique of offering citizenship and generalships to the "Barbarians", the ruse that served Rome so well for so long.

In the 60s, my father bought a new TV set, a Philco. It had two buttons: one for the Christian Democrat Channel, the other for the Socialist Channel. They were ruling together, as partners in the same coalition. Two channels, yes, but the same pro-government song.

And when the time came, in the 70s, to lure even more "Barbarians" into the fold, to enlist the help of the only true opposition into the great power-sharing scheme, the Communists, the scheme was obvious: another slice of the ever-growing media pie. A third network was created, within the vast bosom of RAI and the endless vaults of the public's monies, and it was reserved for the PCI, the Communist Party. The Cold War was fading, the PCI was no longer the "Italian Section" of Stalin's *Internationale* and nothing like a few good jobs, some TV stardom and a media sandlot to play with your friends and comrades works as well to keep even the former "revolutionaries" happy and quiet. And so it did: the Communist had their own little TV network, paid for by the taxpayers of Italy through RAI, of course, and the Cold War, in Italy, was, for all practical purposes, over long before Reagan and Gorbachev tore down that Wall . The Third Channel railed and whined against the bourgeoisie and the imperialists of course, but their revolutionary spirit was confined to TV studios and talk shows.

And just in case they started to take themselves too seriously and make serious troubles, RAI had a solution. For inexplicable "technical" reasons, reception of the Third Network, the so called "red channel" signal, was never as good as that of the other two. And the reached audience was, naturally, a lot smaller. The same RAI technicians who never had any trouble making the first and second channel signals perfectly visible in the remotest valleys of the Alps and lonely islands of the Mediterranean Sea, somehow never quite got around to solving the problem of the Communist channel signal. It invariably suffered from poor reception. Mysteries of the electronic netherworld!

TV had finally become what the printed media already was: a well-partitioned, well-shared consensus machine, conceived to keep everybody well-fed and happy, including the Catholic Church and the Vatican who had no TV network of their own but saw their wishes well represented in the media by their friends, the Christian Democrats.

The so-called "moral doctrines" of the Church, from sex to divorce to abortion, were fully accepted by the mainstream media and by the major TV channels, the Communist included.

The attractive female dancers in variety shows had to wear longjohns under their short skirts, because, as the Chairman of RAI in the 60s himself admitted in his memoirs, the Vatican so desired. Writers of "made-for-TV fiction" had to have their texts formally reviewed by censors with sharp scissors. TV shows were forbidden to mention the words "bed" and "bedroom", because those words could conjure up images that did not have anything to do with sleep (to be fair, even Lucille Ball and Desi Arnaz originally had to have separate beds in their fictitious bedroom, even though they were married).

Divorce and conjugal separations always had to be depicted as enormous tragedies, if they could not be avoided at all. No happiness nor salvation outside the traditional family was possible, and the word abortion was taboo. Mike Bongiorno, a famous and beloved TV personality and host of the number one quiz show in the 50s, temporarily lost his job when a female contestant lost all of her money by wrongly guessing a question whose answer involved the Italian equivalent of the word 'dick' in slang.. In disappointment he blurted out, on live TV and in front of a national audience: 'Oh, my God *signora,* you lost everything for dick'. It took weeks of explanations, replays and abject apologies to convince the "higher authorities" and the *Monsignori* that the poor man meant no crude *double entendre* and his was only an unfortunate lapse.

The censors didn't even spare the ancient and very Italian art of puppeteering. One of the rubber marionettes in a popular puppet show called *Topo Gigio*, "Gigio the Mouse," had to be eliminated from the script because his nose was long, round and bulbous and reminded the censors too much of a penis. I still remember my father, who wrote for that show, shaking his head in disbelief and disgust when he was told to expunge the "phallic" character from his script.

The most insidious and pervasive form of censorship, however, was not as funny or as grotesque as these anecdotes might indicate. And it was not from without, despite the clumsiness of the censors, it was from within. We were the sentinels of ourselves. We were our own censors. We did not dare push the envelope of freedom of the press that, at least on paper and in theory, we had.

In exchange for conformity and complicity, journalist were, for decades after the War, very well treated, according to an age-old, sad truth: the richer the Media, the poorer the Democracy. Following in the steps traced by Mussolini — a journalist himself and thus very well aware of how to treat his former colleagues — the new "democratic governments" of Italy showered the press with enormous benefits and favors. Jobs were made secure for life, thanks to a national and unionized contract. Firing a reporter was practically impossible for a publisher. Raises were automatic and generous every year. Benefits, from lavish pensions payable at age 55 to all sorts of medical coverage for journalists and their families, were incredibly lavish: a journalist was entitled to a private room in any private hospital he or she chose, for free, and to the physician or specialist of his or her choice. No socialized medicine for the boys and girls in the media gravy bus.

The corruption of the independent press went from the brazen to the ridiculous. Professional journalists enjoyed special fares and discounts on everything from airplanes to railroads, from clothing to movie theaters, under the pretense of "doing their job". Even spouses and children were entitled, for obscure "public interest reasons", to a number of free trips on national railroads. Foreign correspondents, supposedly the cream of the crop, were entitled to three, count them, three years advance notice if the home office ever decided to move them to another post or to recall them, even if they had displayed utter incompetence. Unionization of the profession became so pervasive and so suffocating that even editors could not edit one single word in any piece — no matter how awfully written — without the explicit consent of the author, and I mean one single word literally.

And, if and when a new managing editor was appointed by the owners and he — always a he — decided to change the political slant and biases of that paper, a reporter had the right to sue the publisher for damages to his reputation and his "ideology", and collect at least fifteen full months of salary as compensation — no joke.

It would have taken heroes to refuse such officially sanctioned bribery and to rock the boat that carried us all, Communists, right wingers, liberals, conservatives, socialists, so comfortably in life. Besides, one could not even publish a street rag, or start a broadcast station without the permission of, and without belonging to, a professional guild. Only if and when all the "stamps of approval" were given, could the publications be entitled to the State's financial support.

Italy was for four decades proof that legal freedom of the press does not necessarily translate into a free press. And in the late 70s, when journalists were beginning to feel restless and new media were advancing, a wave of political terrorism, of political violence, hit the country, sending everyone scurrying back to the old way of doing business. Just when the Cold War and the Red Threat were receding, freeing a new generation of young reporters eager to trade their "freebies" for "freedom", just when the Communists were no longer seen as a menace to the Constitution, the Red Brigades, with their machine guns and blind violence, resurrected the old ghosts that had kept the Italian media quiet for so long: the ghosts of a violent, bloody revolution.

Never mind the fact that no revolution had ever succeeded in the history of the nation, and even Mussolini took Rome in 1922 with the tacit acknowledgment of the King, the Army, and the very government that he planned to overtake. The phantom menace of the Red Brigades, at best a couple of thousand wide-eyed, unemployed pseudo-intellectuals with too much time and too many guns at their disposal, was enough to frighten the media and force us to act irresponsibly; i.e. to keep quiet.

How could one expose the corruption, the inefficiency, the backwardness of the government, the bureaucracies, the big corporations, and the growing inequality of income and hope, if those were exactly the things that the armed killers were preaching? How could one risk being accused of playing into the hands of those idiots who were shooting down politicians, corporate officers, police and — final proof of their idiocy — even journalists? As so often happens with so-called revolutionary movements, the Red Brigades and their imitators only succeeded in freezing the social situation, thereby slowing the progress of civil liberties in Italy.

Slowing it, but not stopping it. Despite the bloody spasms of the last remnants of the true Marxist faithful, and the opposing, mirror-like violence of minor Neo-Fascist terrorists, Italian society was maturing and the media, perhaps belatedly, reacted. New mastheads appeared, new dailies were launched, in the late 70s and early 80s, in Rome and in Milan. Not by chance did new branches of journalism flourish out of the old tree of lively weekly magazines.

In Rome, Eugenio Scalfari, who for years had published the best of the political weeklies, *L'Espresso,* created a small newspaper called *La Repubblica* to serve the needs of the vast majority of Italians who considered themselves *liberals,* even *leftists* or *Communists,* but could no longer tolerate the rigid, stony propaganda of the old Communist Party. *La Repubblica* was named after the socialist daily in Portugal, assaulted and destroyed by the Portuguese Communists. So timely was Scalfari's intuition, so well-tuned was his paper to the new generations of Italians no longer contented to play their part in the political Operetta, that *La Repubblica* became in ten years the number one newspaper in the country, easily overtaking in the mid-80s the venerable and stale *Corriere della Sera* of Milan. An historic feat that not even Mussolini with his party paper, *Il Popolo d'Italia,* had achieved when he was in control of the whole nation and could ram it down everybody's throat at will.

On the other side of the political spectrum, a moderate right, off-center daily was founded in Milan by a well respected senior journalist, Indro Montanelli, to do on the right wing what *La Repubblica* was doing on the left. Although never as successful, his creation, *Il Giornale,* became an important new voice in the media play. Unfortunately, *Il Giornale* has now become the voice of a new political party, the right, off-center *Forza Italia,* and is falling back into the old rut of Italian journalism: writing under the influence. The party leader's younger brother owns the newspaper.

*S. Berlusconi*

By far the most important development of the late 70s and the early 80s in the realm of politics and media was, however, the collapse of the state monopoly on broadcasting, brought about by a young and ambitious man whose name was destined to become famous: Silvio Berlusconi.

His has been an extraordinary "Italian story", both exciting and depressing in its representation of how the new Italy and the old one can survive arm-in-arm at the same time. Silvio Berlusconi is the son of a modest banker in Milan who left him some capital when he died. In a somewhat surprising and meteoric ascent that has left many critics, and a few district attorneys, wondering, Berlusconi parlayed a small inheritance into a real estate empire, building a string of "satellite cities" around Milan for the baby boomers, who were tired of crowded downtowns. His was the Italian version of the American suburban dream, but with a singular twist.

As a selling point, among scores of similar, cookie-cutter exurbias, Berlusconi created a gimmick: he wired his "satellite cities" with TV cables, in order to give his buyers an extra channel, beyond the offerings of the three RAI channels. It was a private arrangement, a jury-rigged local, cable TV station that broadcast pirated US movies and whatever video cassettes he could get his hands on from a "video room" somewhere in the basement, but it was unmistakably a breach of the existing monopoly.

Many other entrepreneurs had tried to establish "private" channels in the '70s, and all had failed when the lower courts struck them down.

But Berlusconi was not technically "broadcasting". He was "cable-casting" privately only to his home owners, and this was presenting a new challenge to the State-controlled system. And when he was brought to Court and his fledgling cable TV business closed down, he refused to bow down. The case went all the way to the *Corte Costituzionale*, Italy's Supreme Court, and the Justices came back with an astonishing finding. They found that nowhere did the Italian Constitution say that a specific broadcast monopoly was reserved for the State, and in a country where anything not explicitly forbidden is implicitly permissible that was enough to open the floodgates.

Privately owned and operated TV stations sprang up like flowers in a drought-stricken desert after a big rain and with about the same life expectancy. Anybody with an antenna, a transmitter and a few watts of electricity started broadcasting in the late 70s. Pirated movies, porno flicks, strip shows (enormously successful after years of long johns and censored phallic noses), talk shows, sport shows, religious ceremonies, and homemade news shows won viewers who were sick and tired of watching the state-sanctioned and politically controlled channels.

Overnight, viewers went from "dancers in longjohns" to "the homemakers' strip shows" where amateurs exotic dancers bared it all for money and 15 minutes of fame. News went from the "all's well in Italy" message of RAI to the "all's a disaster" cry of the newborn TV stations fighting for survival and advertisers' money to stay afloat. It was chaos, and it was fun. Scores of young people anxious to try their hand at reporting, but barred by the petrified, closed door world of Italian journalism, created amateurish evening news shows, and a new generation of reporters was born.

It was all very Italian. There was no law regulating the air waves, no limits, no anything beyond the ambiguous findings of the Supreme Court — just the freedom to experiment and fail. In the telling idiom of the moment, private TV stations were called free stations.

They soon were not. Out of this primordial broth of media life in the 70s and 80s, only one mastodon emerged and survived: Berlusconi. Other creatures tried and failed. He bought out the better ones, went for the lowest denominator kind of TV: variety shows, quizzes, vaudeville, popular movies, soaps, everything that the lazy, haughty state channels avoided. He understood the immense power of sports, the new "opium of the people", and with the capital accumulated in his real estate boom, bought one of Italy's most adored and dilapidated soccer franchises, A.C. Milan. He invested lavishly to create a dominant team, as a reflection of his ambitions and as a perfect tool for ratings. He behaved like an Italian Citizen Kane, creating an empire out of thin air, admired and hated equally by millions.

But the operative word was "Italian". Berlusconi did it "the Italian way". He knew that for all his monies, and sport laurels, and hot selling subdivisions, to stay in business and to succeed in the end he would need the help and complicity of politicians. He begged at the doors of the dominant Christian Democrats, who were too happy and fat with the State monopoly and too short sighted to understand the new phenomenon. He got the cold shoulder treatment.

He then knocked at the door of the up and coming Socialists, the junior members of the ruling coalition, who were eager to oblige and help Berlusconi grow as an alternative to RAI. In sum, Berlusconi the "media maverick", the creator of the brave new world of communications, grew with new business acumen applied to the old fashioned way: with the patronage of politicians. Promptly a very convenient law was approved with the help of the Socialists and their leader Bettino Craxi, a close Berlusconi friend. A scandalous law that formalized a TV "duopoly" in Italy: three national networks for the State, three national networks for Berlusconi.

The Oligarchs and the Mandarins of the Ancient Regime thought themselves very smart: they had succeeded in co-opting and de-fanging even this aggressive new "Barbarian" at the gate, letting him into the same old cozy arrangement that had served them so well for so long: they sliced the pie of power to feed another client, but kept control of the kitchen.

Except for one thing: the kitchen of power was about to go up in flames. The arrangement might have worked had a number of District Attorneys and Public Prosecutors in Italy not decided at the beginning of the '90s, that enough was enough, and dishonest politicians on the make had to be exposed and prosecuted. Since almost everybody was on the make — two hundred members of Parliament, including Ministers of State, Party leaders and Prime Ministers were indicted as a rush of bribers and bribees turned state evidence — the citadel of power crumbled and in the midst of the ruins, only Berlusconi stood, with his by now untouchable media empire intact.

Instead of playing the role of the former barbarian who becomes the protector of Rome, Berlusconi turned out to be the proverbial Trojan Horse. It did not take much for such a shrewd and able salesman to understand that the media empire he controlled could become, in the age of television, an instant political empire.

Seeing the collapse of his political sponsors and protectors, like Bettino Craxi, and suspecting (not without reason) that the magistrates were maneuvered by "a vast left wing conspiracy" led by the now former but still formidable Communists, (nothing new under the sun, when it comes to political conspiracy theorists) Berlusconi once again looked for an "Italian" solution. He would become his own protector, his own political shield,. He would transform his media empire into a political force. Media and politics merged into one, single, formidable force.

His TV world became a party, a new kind of political party, without members, rallies, leaflets, but with a lot more than contributions and phony, adoring conventions: a 50 percent share of the Italian TV audience. His three TV channels became a permanent convention, bombarding the public with daily, even hourly, stupefying propaganda such as Italy had never seen before and America is so well used to: the propaganda of klieg lights, political spots, happy faces and cheap promises, the "huff and puff and fluff" of today's infomercialized and lamentable political life.

Berlusconi gave the Italians what they wanted, happy, entertaining, fat-free and thought-free TV in exchange for their votes, and he got those votes in droves. In 1994 Berlusconi, a person who had never run for public office, won a national election and became Prime Minister for a few months, before being scuttled by the classical Italian internal conspiracy. And in 2001 he is, according to the polls, poised to win back the job overwhelmingly.

The media had finally and truly become the message. The apparent separation of Media and Politics had crumbled, revealing the sad truth with glaring clarity. The "Party Line," toed once on the Left, was not the real of the Right, but the substance was identical: a Media enlisted for explicit political purpose.

The rest of the journalists who were supposed to mediate between the political lies and the truth found themselves too discredited, too far behind the curve to counter Berlusconi's ruthless propaganda. After too many years of half truths, of outright lies, of blatant sucking up to powerful politicians, we had our comeuppance. When we started crying wolf," nobody believed us. And it was easy, and perhaps fair, for the Legionnaires of the Berlusconi Party to remind their adversaries of their own sins: we are doing what you did for years on the other side, or on the side of the government.

Journalists in Italy had played the game of power for too long to be credible when the time came to denounce the risks of political Tele-evangelism as practiced by Berlusconi.

The same sad old pantomime of role-playing and finding new patrons is now more modern, but even more rampant. Former so-called liberal writers and TV media personalities are now currying favor with the "New Emperor", like defeated legionnaires in ancient Rome, switching loyalties. Few and far between papers and voices are trying to stay independent. If they do, they are denounced as Communist by Berlusconi, with the same venomous bile that Communists employed to dismiss any opponent in the past as fascist.

And the old curse of Italian journalism has proven itself true again. Those who work for Berlusconi are now free to attack the ruling government as long as their "Godfather" does not become *the* government. When that will happen, they will be "free" to support the new Prime Minister and will be "free" to attack the new majority. The Opera continues, as a made for TV Soap Opera.

## NEW JOURNALISM

To try and save themselves from the curse of politically

apportioned journalism (an oxymoron, if one ever existed), new generations of reporters have resigned themselves to taking refuge, in Italy as well as here in the Unites States, in what has been called "new journalism", the reporting of light news, fluffy features, human angle stories, celebrities, and crime boilerplates that readers and viewers apparently lap up. Coverage of politics is more and more coverage of politicians, of their families, of their private and public kisses, and less and less of ideas. We spend more time and energy trying to find out with whom a politician goes to bed, than with what ideas he wakes up in the morning.

For circulation and for ratings' sake, or for the sake of quiet living, we are the hostages of "fluff"; used as an alibi for our timidity.

I vividly remember when I first moved to Washington D.C. to become the chief of the U.S. bureau for *La Stampa* of Turin, how excited and heartened I was at discovering American journalism first hand, after so many years of play-acting in Italy. It was 1973 and the Beltway cauldron was bubbling in the maelstrom of the Watergate affair. American papers and electronic media seemed, to a young foreign journalist, everything that journalism should be and most assuredly was not in Italy and, by and large, in Europe. Yes, they were biased; yes, they made mistakes; yes, they were superficial and glib and all hated Richard Nixon, but the boys and girls at the *Washington Post,* at the *NY Times,* at *CBS,* at *AP* and *UPI* knew what a real story was, what a journalist's job in a free society was. Measuring our way of "writing under the influence" against the "American way" of serving the public's needs gave me hope.

How disappointing it was, when I came back to America in the 80s, to discover that the gap between the "Italian way" and the "American way" had narrowed dramatically. News outlets and shows in the U.S. appeared to be more and more partisan and politically recognizable, like Italian news outlets. TV, cable, and even Internet news all seemed to have become part of the "Entertainment and Marketing" division of their respective controlling corporations. Serious and consistent coverage of foreign stories had all but disappeared, with very few exceptions, and the mantra of "new journalism" had become synonymous with "no journalism".

Perhaps this is the just by-product of the "death of ideologies", of the age of the single and unifying thought that leaves no room for serious debate outside of the Dow Jones Index and the sex life of celebrities, and this too shall pass. And by no means do I want to come across to you as an aging curmudgeon who waxes nostalgic over the way things were. I enjoy a juicy, dirty sex scandal in the White House like the next person, and things, for us in the Italian media, are a lot better today than they were yesterday.

It is what I see happening in the U.S. media that worries me, because the U.S. Media is, more than ever, the standard by which the rest of the world's media measures itself, including those who refuse at admit it. I see the self-censorship under the guise of "fairness", the intellectual timidity dressed up as "political correctness", the obsessive "role playing" exemplified in the phony TV debates where the left and right, the liberal and the conservative, the pro-life and the pro-choice all play their part, sing their expected song, pick up the check and leave for the next show.

I still remember with a shudder my appearance in a Crossfire show, during a Middle East hostage crisis that involved Italy. One of the two hosts warned me beforehand, in the pre-interview, that he would severely scold Italy and its government for their complicity with the Palestinian terrorists and the "wink and nod" attitude toward rogue states like Libya. I agreed with him wholeheartedly. 'For Christ's sake, Vittorio, are you out of your mind?' shouted my terrified host: 'You HAVE to disagree with me, yell at me, get mad at me for insulting your government and your country. This is a show, a SHOW, do you understand?'.

I understood. Suddenly I was brought back to the Italy of the opera, to the stilted, pre-cooked debates where we all had to play our part, to say our "thing". I had a flashback to my years in Rome and the insistent, anxious questions of my colleagues, unsettled by a newcomer without a clear label on his forehead: tell us what you are. Are you a Commie, a Socialist, a Liberal, what are you?

The Germans have a word for it: it's called *schadefreude*, the malicious joy of seeing somebody else's downfall. But I'm not happy. I'm not proud to see American journalism become day after day more and more similar to ours, by descending and condescending, by unconsciously chasing consensus at the expense of dissent. If I warn you, it is not because I know better, it is simply because I know: I have seen the dangers of your future in our past.

## ABOUT THE AUTHORS

Giannandrea Falchi is a graduate in Economics and Statistics of the University of Rome and studied also at the London School of Economics and Political Science. Currently he is the Representative of Banca d'Italia (Italian Central Bank) in the United States, as well as Observer for Canada and Mexico. Previously, Falchi was an economist in the Research Department of Banca d'Italia in Rome (1976-88), Member of the OECD's Financial Market Committee in Paris (1982-88), Economic adviser to the Italian Minister for Foreign Trade in Rome (1987-88), Representative of Banca d'Italia and Financial Attache of the Italian Embassy in Paris (1993-97).

He is the author of a number of essays on the functioning of the International Monetary System. Among them: *"L'Italie et La Monnaie Unique,"* Institut des Haute Etudes de Defence Nationale, Athena, 1997 (Paris: la Documentation Francaise). *"La Borsa di Londra"* (The British Stock Market) (Rome, Bancaria). *"The Glass-Stea gal Act"* (Fondazione A. Olivetti, 1989). *"The Role of Gold in Central Bank's Reserves"* (Oxford: Oxford University Press, 1982).

Maria Elisabetta de Franciscis has lectured extensively on Italian politics, history and the Italian Constitution, in both Italian and American institutions and at international symposia. She is the author of *Italy and the Vatican: The 1984 Concordat between Church and State* (1989) and *Il Presidente degli Stati Uniti d'America: Costituzione e Prassi"* (1996).

She has co-authored with Mary L. Volcannsek and Jacquelin Lucienne Lafon *Judicial Misconduct. A Cross National Comparison* (1996), and has contributed to such works as: *Il decentramento politico negli Stati dell'Unione Europea* (1996), *Judicial Making in Europe* (1992), *Political Leaders of Contemporary Western Europe* (1995), *Women in Law* (1996) and *Italy in Transition* (1997). Currently she teaches Constitutional Law at the University Federico II, Naples, Italy.

Maristella de Panizza Lorch, a native of Bolzano, Italy, has been a tenured member for 40 years in Italian and Medieval-

Renaissance Studies at Columbia University. Director of the "Casa Italiana" at Columbia, she personally introduced Fellini, Visconti, Rossellini and Italian neo-realistic movie directors to American audience.

As founder and Director of the Center of Italian Studies at Barnard and the School of International Affairs (1976-90), of the Center for Medieval and Renaissance Studies (1976) and of the Center for International Scholarly Exchanges (1980-90) she played a crucial role in promoting Italian studies in America.

She was the founding Director of "The Italian Academy for Advanced Studies in America," established in New York in 1991 to provide a privileged vision of Europe from an Italian perspective through Colombia University. Her books and articles published in Italian and American Journals reflect her cultural as well as political interests in Italian political life.

Vittorio Zucconi was born 55 years ago in Modena, Italy, the land of fast cars, repentant communists and delicious high cholesterol foods. He graduated *summa cum laude* in Modern History from the University of Milan. He tried his hand at College teaching, but claims that it was to his students' great relief, that he moved out of Academia to work in journalism. He has been a professional journalist for the last 30 years.

As a foreign correspondent, he represented all the major Italian dailies: *La Stampa, Il Corriere della Sera, La Repubblica*, in Bruxelles, Moscow, Paris, Tokyo and now in Washington, and has covered more wars, unrest, scandals, crises and US presidential elections than he cares to remember.

He has conducted several TV shows and has published books on Russia, Japan, United States and journalism, some of which have been best sellers. But the book of which he is proudest is a collection of short stories on racism and intolerance, now adopted by Italian High Schools as a writing and reading text. He has been married to Alisa Tibaldi for 32 years and their two children, Chiara and Guido, are both graduates of US Colleges.

# INDEX

## A

Agreement 9, 12, 22, 27, 31, 33, 34, 41, 43, 60, 105, 112
Albertine Statute 9, 25, 43, 50, 52
Alema 1, 2, 13
America 3, 6, 15, 18, 24, 28, 40, 51, 59-61, 63, 83-85, 88-89, 91, 95-96, 116, 122, 124, 130, 133, 135-136, 139-140
Andreotti 1, 54, 60, 122-123
Arbasino 4, 59-60, 76, 82-83, 90
Ariosto 4, 60-61, 67-76, 96, 98

## B

Bank 1-2, 5, 35, 49, 69, 107, 109-112, 130, 139
Berlusconi 1, 130-134
Bicameral Committee 9, 13-14, 17
Boccaccio 62
Boiardo 67, 68, 69, 70
Branch 3-4, 7-10, 15-17, 22, 24, 30-32, 34, 38-40, 44, 109, 111, 129

## C

Calvino 59-62, 67, 72, 89, 90, 96-98
Catholicism 97
Censor 126, 127, 131, 136
Chamber of Deputies 17, 43, 46, 48, 53
Channel 12, 56, 123-126, 130
Charter 41
Choice 10, 13, 17, 81, 124, 127, 136
Christian Democrat 1, 19, 98, 122, 125, 127-128, 134
Ciampi 1, 4, 18-19, 32, 35, 40, 54, 56
Circulation 121, 123, 135
CISE 95
Civil Law 4, 9, 29, 39, 41, 56
Common Law 4, 9, 39, 40-41, 56-57
Communism 97
Communist 1, 89-90, 119-121, 125-126, 128-129, 133-134, 140
Competition 45, 104, 106, 108-112
Constituent Assembly 8-11, 17-20, 22, 24-26, 30-31, 37, 42, 44, 50-52

Constitution iii, 3, 4, 7-42, 44-57, 119, 128, 131, 139
Cossiga 19, 25, 28, 32-33, 36, 38, 51, 54, 60
Council of Ministers 7, 10-11, 13, 24, 27, 31, 34-35, 44, 48
Coup 5, 8, 12, 30, 60, 71, 77, 89, 104, 129
Court 1, 4, 8, 14, 23-25, 27-28, 39-41, 45, 48, 51-52, 68-71, 74, 79, 118, 124, 131
Court of Cassation 23
Craxi 93, 122-123, 132-133
Crisis 11, 33, 35-37, 39, 67, 83, 122, 136, 140
Cult ii

**D**

Dante 4, 60-67, 72-76, 84, 98
De Mita 13
Debate 4-5, 28, 32, 34, 41, 45, 48-49, 53, 56, 60, 62, 69, 76, 82, 85-87, 89-91, 94, 97, 101, 136
Defense 16, 24, 40, 88, 90, 92, 100
Deliberation 28, 49
Democracy 3-4, 11-12, 22, 25, 39, 42, 116-117, 120, 127
Dependency 121
Development 7-8, 9, 12, 37, 70, 71, 72, 73, 106, 116, 130
Dini 35, 59, 95
Dissolve 22, 26-27, 31, 36-37, 50, 55
Divinity 61, 63

**E**

Economy i-iii, 2, 5, 103-107, 112
Einaudi 3, 37
Electoral College 17-18
EMU 6, 103, 110, 112
Entrepreneur 108, 112, 131
Este 68, 70-71
Euro i, iii, 1, 5-6, 9, 32, 40-43, 46-47, 52, 56-57, 61, 103-105, 108-114, 116, 135, 139-140
European Monetary Union 1, 5, 103
Exile 65

**F**

Faith 64, 90, 121-122, 129

Falchi iii, 2, 5, 103, 139
Fascism 5, 82, 89, 97, 119-120
Ferrara 68, 70-71
Filippo 59, 88
Finance 5-6, 14, 26, 88, 103, 107, 110-112, 115, 117, 121, 128, 139
Florence 65, 66, 93
Folly 67-74, 100
Forza Italia 1, 130
Franciscis iii, 2-3, 7, 42-43, 45, 47, 50, 56-57, 139
Freedom 6, 30, 50, 57, 68, 87, 110, 116-117, 119-121, 123, 127-128, 131

**G**

GDP 5, 103, 104, 106-108
Genre 69, 76, 83-85, 97
God 64-66, 68-69, 71, 73-74, 121, 123, 127, 134

**H**

Heaven 62-63, 65
Hell 62, 73
Higher education 3, 39
Honors 25
Humanism 4, 67

**I**

Il Giorno 117, 118
Immigrant 2
Impegno 61, 88, 92-93
Independence 6, 15, 19, 71, 91, 117
Influence iii, 6-7, 31, 54, 113, 118, 119, 130, 135
Insanity 67, 70, 71, 72, 74, 75, 100
Investment 5, 104, 106, 108-110, 112

**J**

Janni i, 6, 42, 60
Jotti 13

Journalism i-iii, 6, 113, 115-117, 121-122, 129-131, 134-136, 140
Judiciary 14-16, 24, 27-28, 32-33, 38, 48-49, 51, 56, 77
Jurisprudence 40, 117

**K**

King 9-10, 21-22, 30, 43, 50, 65, 70, 80, 108, 111, 117-118, 129
Kosovo 2

**L**

Law 3-4, 9-16, 18, 20-23, 25, 27-29, 31-32, 35-36, 38-51, 55-57, 84, 106, 108, 113, 119, 122, 124-125, 131-132, 139
Levi 89, 94
Library ii
Life Senator 28
Light/Dark 2, 4, 15, 36, 61-62, 65-68, 72-74, 81-82, 85, 97, 105, 108, 113, 133, 135
Literature i-iii, 4, 59-62, 65-68, 72, 76, 79, 80-83, 85, 87-96, 100-101
Lorch iii, 2, 4, 59, 66, 100, 139

**M**

Mafia 1, 93, 98
Magazines 123-124, 129
Market 2, 5, 6, 45, 105, 103, 105-112, 122, 135, 139
Mattei 117
McLean i, 6
Media 1, 3, 14, 39, 45, 54, 114, 117, 119, 120, 121, 123-136
Minorities 13, 17, 46
Missiroli 115
Mood 2, 61, 68, 88
Moral 11, 66, 74, 93, 95, 126
Multipartitism 8, 13, 47
Mussolini 8, 118, 124, 127, 129-130
Myth 62, 66-72, 98-100

**N**

NATO 2, 41, 120
Neorealistic 61, 82, 94, 140

Newspapers 115, 120-121, 123
Noir 4, 60, 84, 85, 86, 101
Novel 4, 15, 60, 76-78, 81-86, 89-90, 92, 94-95, 98

**O**

Occupation 88, 92

**P**

Palermo 1, 91
Paradise 62, 65-66
Pardon 10, 25, 49-50
Parliament 1, 3-4, 7-8, 10-13, 15-22, 26-27, 30-37, 39-42, 44-46, 51, 54-55, 57, 133
Participatory 3, 25, 30, 39
Party 1, 13, 16, 18-19, 93, 98, 119-122, 124-125, 129-130, 133-134
Pasolini 76-77, 92
Passion 5, 68, 70-71, 73, 75, 84-85, 97-98
Peace 2, 8, 14, 17, 24, 39, 47, 68, 70-71
Peaceful revolution 8, 14, 17, 39
Pendulum 4, 30, 39-40
Pertini 33, 38, 54, 93, 122
Perugia 1
Pilgrim 73-74
Pope 43, 65, 69-71, 117-118
Post-war 88-89, 117, 119, 124
Post-war Italy iii, 6, 113
Power to manifest 33-34, 38
Powers 3-4, 7-11, 14-17, 20-31, 34-35, 37-40, 43-44, 48, 50, 53-55, 120
Praxis iii, 3, 7, 17, 28-30, 32, 37, 42
Premises 7, 62, 95
Presidency iii, 3, 7-8, 13, 17, 19, 28-29, 32
President 1, 3-4, 7-9, 11, 13-15, 17-38, 40, 42, 44, 46-56, 122, 139-140
Prodi 1, 13, 44, 75
Productivity 3, 39, 106, 112
Punishment 10, 25, 50, 55
Purgatory 62, 73

**R**

RAI 124-126, 130-132
Reference ii
Regional Councils 18, 26, 46
Regionalism 8, 26, 57
Regulations 13, 15-16, 49, 104, 108-109, 111
Renaissance 4, 60, 63, 66-67, 79, 100, 140
Republic 1, 3-4, 7-8, 10-15, 17-38, 40, 42, 44, 46-56, 70, 86, 116
Resistance 30, 88-89
Risorgimento 30

**S**

Saint Thomas 63
Satellite 130
Savings 111, 112
Scalfaro 3, 33, 35, 37, 48, 53-55, 85
School 3, 31, 39, 97, 114, 139-140
Sciascia 5, 84, 93, 96-100
Securities 108
Self-employment 105
Sinful 68
Skepticism 14, 90
Socialist 93, 122, 125, 128-129, 132, 136
Society iii, 2, 4, 59-85, 88-89, 91-92, 97, 100-101, 116, 129, 135
Sovereign 7, 13, 17, 32, 34, 40, 41, 44, 56-57
Stewardship 38-39
Subsidy 121
Suffrage 10, 43

**T**

Tabucchi 59, 84-85
Technical 35, 54, 60, 112, 126, 131
Theme 62, 79, 86, 89-90, 92, 95-96
Transition iii, 3, 7-8, 11, 14-17, 23, 26, 28-30, 34, 37-39, 42, 45, 49, 54, 56, 119, 139
Treaty 41, 43
TV 116, 123-127, 130-136, 140

**U**

Unemployment 2, 104-106, 129
Union 2, 6, 9, 41, 43, 46, 52, 56-57, 103-105, 112, 127-128, 139
United States 6, 16, 18, 20, 24, 28, 40, 47, 51, 57, 104, 108, 113, 117, 121-122, 139-140
Unrequited love 68, 74

**V**

Valla 69, 100
Value ii
Violence 84-85, 93, 128-129

**W**

Walsh 6
Wealth 43, 91
Women 22, 25, 43, 59, 82-83, 95, 113, 117-118, 123, 139
Writing under the Influence iii, 6, 113, 118, 130, 135

**Y**

Yugoslavia 2, 119

**Z**

Zucconi iii, 2, 6, 113, 140

# THE COUNCIL FOR RESEARCH IN VALUES AND PHILOSOPHY

## PURPOSE

Today there is urgent need to attend to the nature and dignity of the person, to the quality of human life, to the purpose and goal of the physical transformation of our environment, and to the relation of all this to the development of social and political life. This, in turn, requires philosophic clarification of the base upon which freedom is exercised, that is, of the values which provide stability and guidance to one's decisions.

Such studies must be able to reach deeply into the cultures of one's nation--and of other parts of the world by which they can be strengthened and enriched--in order to uncover the roots of the dignity of persons and of the societies built upon their relations one with another. They must be able to identify the conceptual forms in terms of which modern industrial and technological developments are structured and how these impact human self-understanding. Above all, they must be able to bring these elements together in the creative understanding essential for setting our goals and determining our modes of interaction. In the present complex circumstances this is a condition for growing together with trust and justice, honest dedication and mutual concern.

The Council for Studies in Values and Philosophy (RVP) is a group of scholars who share the above concerns and are interested in the application thereto of existing capabilities in the field of philosophy and other disciplines. Its work is to identify areas in which study is needed, the intellectual resources which can be brought to bear thereupon, and the means for publication and interchange of the work from the various regions of the world. In bringing these together its goal is scientific discovery and publication which contributes to the promotion of human kind in our times.

In sum, our times present both the need and the opportunity for deeper and ever more progressive understanding of the person and of the foundations of social life. The development of such understanding is the goal of the RVP.

## PROJECTS

A set of related research efforts is currently in process; some were developed initially by the RVP and others now are being carried forward by it, either solely or conjointly.

1. *Cultural Heritage and Contemporary Change: Philosophical Foundations for Social Life.* Sets of focused and mutually coordinated continuing seminars in university centers, each preparing a volume as part of an integrated philosophic search for self-understanding differentiated by continent. This work focuses upon evolving a more adequate understanding of the person in society and looks to the cultural heritage of each for the resources to respond to the challenges of its own specific contemporary transformation.

2. *Seminars on Culture and Contemporary Issues.* This series of 10 week cross-cultural and inter-disciplinary seminars is being coordina-ted by the RVP in Washington.

3. *Joint-Colloquia* with Institutes of Philosophy of the National Academies of Science, university philosophy departments, and societies, which have been underway since 1976 in Eastern Europe and, since 1987 in China, concern the person in contemporary society.

4. *Foundations of Moral Education and Character Development.* A study in values and education which unites philosophers, psychologists, social scientists and scholars in education in the elaboration of ways of enriching the moral content of education and character development. This work has been underway since 1980 especially in the Americas.

The personnel for these projects consists of established scholars willing to contribute their time and research as part of their professional commitment to life in our society. For resources to implement this work the Council, as a non-profit organization incorporated in the District of Colombia, looks to various private foundations, public programs and enterprises.

## PUBLICATIONS ON CULTURAL HERITAGE AND CONTEMPORARY CHANGE

| | |
|---|---|
| *Series I.* | *Culture and Values* |
| *Series II.* | *Africa* |
| *Series IIa.* | *Islam* |
| *Series III.* | *Asia* |
| *Series IV.* | *W. Europe and North America* |
| *Series IVa.* | *Central and Eastern Europe* |
| *Series V.* | *Latin America* |
| *Series VI.* | *Foundations of Moral Education* |

# CULTURAL HERITAGE AND CONTEMPORARY CHANGE

## VALUES AND CONTEMPORARY LIFE

### Series I. Culture and Values

Vol. I.1 *Research on Culture and Values: Intersection of Universities, Churches and Nations*,
George F. McLean,
ISBN 0-8191-7352-5 (cloth); ISBN 0-8191-7353-3 (paper).
Vol. I.2 *The Knowledge of Values: A Methodological Introduction to the Study of Values*,
A. Lopez Quintas,
ISBN 0-8191-7418-1 (cloth); ISBN 0-8191-7419-x (paper).
Vol. I.3 *Reading Philosophy for the XXIst Century*,
George F. McLean,
ISBN 0-8191-7414-9 (cloth); ISBN 0-8191-7415-7 9paper).
Vol. I.4 *Relations Between Cultures*,
John Kromkowski,
ISBN 1-56518-009-7 (cloth); ISBN 1-56518-008-9 (paper).
Vol. I.5 *Urbanization and Values*,
John Kromkowski,
ISBN 1-56518-011-9 (cloth); ISBN 1-56518-010-0 (paper).
Vol. I.6 *The Place of the Person in Social Life*,
Paul Peachey and John Kromkowski,
ISBN 1-56518-013-5 (cloth); ISBN 1-56518-012-7 (paper).
Vol. I.7 *Abrahamic Faiths, Ethnicity and Ethnic Conflicts*,
Paul Peachey, George F. McLean and John Kromkowski
ISBN 1-56518-104-2 (paper).
Vol. I.8 *Ancient Western Philosophy: The Hellenic Emergence*,
George F. McLean and Patrick J. Aspell
ISBN 1-56518-100-X (paper).
Vol. I. 9 *Medieval Western Philosophy: The European Emergence*,
Patrick J. Aspell
ISBN 1-56518-094-1 (paper).
Vol. I.10 *The Ethical Implications of Unity and the Divine in Nicholas of Cusa*
David L. De Leonardis

ISBN 1-56518-112-3 (paper).

Vol. I.11 *Ethics at the Crossroads: Vol. 1. Normative Ethics and Objective Reason,*
George F. McLean,
ISBN 1-56518-022-4 (paper).

Vol. I.12 *Ethics at the Crossroads: Vol. 2. Personalist Ethics and Human Subjectivity,*
George F. McLean,
ISBN 1-56518-024-0 (paper).

Vol. I.13 *The Emancipative Theory of Jürgen Habermas and Metaphysics,*
Robert Badillo,
ISBN 1-56518-043-7 (cloth); ISBN 1-56518-042-9 (paper).

Vol. I.14 *The Deficient Cause of Moral Evil According to Thomas Aquinas,*
Edward Cook,
ISBN 1-56518-070-4 paper (paper).

Vol. I.16 *Civil Society and Social Reconstruction,*
George F. McLean,
ISBN 1-56518-086-0 (paper).

Vol.I.17 *Ways to God, Personal and Social at the Turn of Millennia The Iqbal Lecture, Lahore*
George F. McLean
ISBN 1-56518-123-9 (paper).

Vol.I.18 *The Role of the Sublime in Kant's Moral Metaphysics*
John R. Goodreau
ISBN 1-56518-124-7 (paper).

Vol.I .20 *Faith, reason and Philosophy*
*Lectures at The al-Azhar, Qum, Tehran, Lahore and Beijing*
*Appendix: The Encyclical Letter: Fides et Ratio*
George F. McLean
ISBN 1-56518-130-1 (paper).

Vol.I.21 *Religion and the Relation between Civilizations: Lectures on Cooperation between Islamic and Christian Cultures in a Global Horizon*
George F. McLean
ISBN 1-56518-152-2 (paper).

Vol.22 F*reedom, Cultural Traditions and Progress: Philosophy in Civil Society and Nation Building:*

*Tashkent Lectures, 1999*
George F. McLean
ISBN 1-56518-151-4 (paper).

## CULTURAL HERITAGES AND THE FOUNDATIONS OF SOCIAL LIFE

### Series II. Africa

Vol. II.1 *Person and Community: Ghanaian Philosophical Studies: I,*
Kwasi Wiredu and Kwame Gyeke,
ISBN 1-56518-005-4 (cloth); ISBN 1-56518-004-6 (paper).
Vol. II.2 *The Foundations of Social Life: Ugandan Philosophical Studies: I,*
A.T. Dalfovo,
ISBN 1-56518-007-0 (cloth); ISBN 1-56518-006-2 (paper).
Vol. II.3 *Identity and Change in Nigeria: Nigerian Philosophical Studies, I,*
Theophilus Okere,
ISBN 1-56518-068-2 (paper).
Vol. II.4 *Social Reconstruction in Africa: Ugandan Philosophical studies, II*
E. Wamala, A.R. Byaruhanga, A.T. Dalfovo,
J.K. Kigongo, S.A. Mwanahewa and G. Tusabe
ISBN 1-56518-118-2 (paper).
Vol. II.5 *Ghana: Changing Values/Chaning Technologies: Ghanaian Philosophical Studies, II*
Helen Lauer
ISBN 1-56518-1441 (paper).
Vol. 11.6 *Sameness and Difference: Problems and Potentials in South African Civil Society: South African Philosophical Studies, I*
James R. Cochrane and Bastienne Klein
ISBN 1-56518-1557 (paper).

### Series IIA. Islam

Vol. IIA.1 *Islam and the Political Order,*
Muhammad Saïd al-Ashmawy,
ISBN 1-56518-046-1 (cloth); ISBN 1-56518-047-x (paper).

Vol. IIA.3 *Philosophy in Pakistan*
Naeem Ahmad
ISBN 1-56518-108-5 (paper).

Vol. IIA.4 *The Authenticity of the Text in Hermeneutics*
Seyed Musa Dibadj
ISBN 1-56518-117-4 (paper).

Vol. IIA.5 *Interpretation and the Problem of the Intention of the Author: H.-G. Gadamer vs E.D. Hirsch*
Burhanettin Tatar
ISBN 1-56518-121 (paper).

Vol.IAI.6 *Ways to God, Personal and Social at the Turn of Millennia The Iqbal Lecture, Lahore*
George F. McLean
ISBN 1-56518-123-9 (paper).

Vol.I .7 *Faith, reason and Philosophy Lectures at The al-Azhar, Qum, Tehran, Lahore and Beijing Appendix: The Encyclical Letter: Fides et Ratio*
George F. McLean
ISBN 1-56518-130-1 (paper).

Vol.IIA.10 *Christian-Islamic Preambles of Faith*
Joseph Kenny
ISBN 1-56518-138-7 (paper).

Vol.IIA.12 *Religion and the Relation between Civilizations: Lectures on Cooperation between Islamic and Christian Cultures in a Global Horizon*
George F. McLean
ISBN 1-56518-152-2 (paper).

## Series III. Asia

Vol. III.1 *Man and Nature: Chinese Philosophical Studies, I,*
Tang Yi-jie, Li Zhen,
ISBN 0-8191-7412-2 (cloth); ISBN 0-8191-7413-0 (paper).

Vol. III.2 *Chinese Foundations for Moral Education and Character Development, Chinese Philosophical Studies, II.*
Tran van Doan,
ISBN 1-56518-033-x (cloth); ISBN 1-56518-032-1 (paper).

Vol. III.3 *Confucianism, Buddhism, Taoism, Christianity and Chinese Culture, Chinese Philosophical Studies, III,*

Tang Yijie,

ISBN 1-56518-035-6 (cloth); ISBN 1-56518-034-8 (paper).

Vol. III.4 *Morality, Metaphysics and Chinese Culture (Metaphysics, Culture and Morality, Vol. I)*
Vincent Shen and Tran van Doan,
ISBN 1-56518-026-7 (cloth); ISBN 1-56518-027-5 (paper).

Vol. III.5 *Tradition, Harmony and Transcendence,*
George F. McLean,
ISBN 1-56518-030-5 (cloth); ISBN 1-56518-031-3 (paper).

Vol. III.6 *Psychology, Phenomenology and Chinese Philosophy: Chinese Philosophical Studies, VI,*
Vincent Shen, Richard Knowles and Tran Van Doan,
ISBN 1-56518-044-5 (cloth); 1-56518-045-3 (paper).

Vol. III.7 *Values in Philippine Culture and Education: Philippine Philosophical Studies, I,*
Manuel B. Dy, Jr.,
ISBN 1-56518-040-2 (cloth); 1-56518-041-2 (paper).

Vol. III.7A *The Human Person and Society: Chinese Philosophical Studies, VIIA,*
Zhu Dasheng, Jin Xiping and George F. McLean
ISBN 1-56518-087-9 (library edition); 1-56518-088-7 (paper).

Vol. III.8 *The Filipino Mind: Philippine Philosophical Studies II,*
Leonardo N. Mercado
ISBN 1-56518-063-1 (cloth); ISBN 1-56518-064-X (paper).

Vol. III.9 *Philosophy of Science and Education: Chinese Philosophical Studies IX,*
Vincent Shen and Tran Van Doan
ISBN 1-56518-075-5 (cloth); 1-56518-076-3 (paper).

Vol. III.10 *Chinese Cultural Traditions and Modernization: Chinese Philosophical Studies, X,*
Wang Miaoyang, Yu Xuanmeng and George F. McLean
ISBN 1-56518-067-4 (library edition); 1-56518-068-2 (paper).

Vol. III.11 *The Humanization of Technology and Chinese Culture: Chinese Philosophical Studies XI,*
Tomonobu Imamichi, Wang Miaoyang and Liu Fangtong
ISBN 1-56518-116-6 (paper).

Vol. III.12 *Beyond Modernization: Chinese Roots of Global Awareness: Chinese Philosophical Studies, XII,*
Wang Miaoyang, Yu Xuanmeng and George F. McLean

ISBN 1-56518-089-5 (library edition); 1-56518-090-9 (paper).

Vol. III.13 *Philosophy and Modernization in China: Chinese Philosophical Studies XIII,*
Liu Fangtong, Huang Songjie and George F. McLean
ISBN 1-56518-066-6 (paper).

Vol. III.14 *Economic Ethics and Chinese Culture: Chinese Philosophical Studies, XIV,*
Yu Xuanmeng, Lu Xiaohe, Liu Fangtong, Zhang Rulun and Georges Enderle
ISBN 1-56518-091-7 (library edition); 1-56518-092-5 (paper).

Vol. III.15 *Civil Society in a Chinese Context: Chinese Philosophical Studies XV,*
Wang Miaoyang, Yu Xuanmeng and Manuel B. Dy
ISBN 1-56518-084-4 (paper).

Vol. III.16 T*he Bases of Values in a Time of Change: Chinese and Western: Chinese Philosophical Studies, XVI*
Kirti Bunchua, Liu Fangtong, Yu Xuanmeng, Yu Wujin
ISBN 1-56518-114-X (paper).

Vol. IIIB.1 *Authentic Human Destiny: The Paths of Shankara and Heidegger*
Vensus A. George
ISBN 1-56518-119-0 (paper).

Vol. IIIB.2 *The experience of being as goal of human existence: the Heideggerian approach*
Vensus A. George
ISBN 1-56518-145-X (paper).

Vol. IIIB.5 *Gandhi: the Meaning of Mahatma for the Millennium Indian Philosophical Studies, II*
Kuruvilla Pandikattu
ISBN 1-56518-156-5 (paper).

Vol. IIIC.1 *Spiritual values and social progress: Uzbekistan Philosophical Studies, I*
Siad Shermukhamedov, Victoriya Levinskaya.
ISBN 1-56518-143-3 (paper).

## Series IV. Western Europe and North America

Vol. IV.1 *Italy in Transition: The Long Road from the First to the Second Republic: The 1997 Edmund D. Pellegrino Lecture*

*on Contemporary Italian Politics*
Paolo Janni
ISBN 1-56518-120-4 (paper).

Vol. IV.2 *Italy and The European Monetary Union: The 1997 Edmund D. Pellegrino Lecture on Contemporary Italian Politics*
Paolo Janni
ISBN 1-56518-128-X (paper).

Vol.IV.3 *Italy at the Millennium: Economy, Politics, Literature and Journalism: The 1999 Edmund D. Pellegrino Lectures on Contemporary Italian Politics*
Paolo Janni
ISBN 1-56518-158-1 (pbk.)

## Series IVA. Central and Eastern Europe

Vol. IVA.1 *The Philosophy of Person: Solidarity and Cultural Creativity: Polish Philosophical Studies, I,*
A. Tischner, J.M. Zycinski,
ISBN 1-56518-048-8 (cloth); ISBN 1-56518-049-6 (paper).

Vol. IVA.2 *Public and Private Social Inventions in Modern Societies: Polish Philosophical Studies, II,*
L. Dyczewski, P. Peachey, J. Kromkowski,
ISBN 1-56518-050-x (cloth). paper ISBN 1-56518-051-8 (paper).

Vol. IVA.3 *Traditions and Present Problems of Czech Political Culture: Czechoslovak Philosophical Studies, I,*
M. Bedná , M. Vejraka
ISBN 1-56518-056-9 (cloth); ISBN 1-56518-057-7 (paper).

Vol. IVA.4 *Czech Philosophy in the XXth Century: Czech Philosophical Studies, II,*
Lubomír Nový and Jirí Gabriel,
ISBN 1-56518-028-3 (cloth); ISBN 1-56518-029-1 (paper).

Vol. IVA.5 *Language, Values and the Slovak Nation: Slovak Philosophical Studies, I,*
Tibor Pichler and Jana Gašparíková,
ISBN 1-56518-036-4 (cloth); ISBN 1-56518-037-2 (paper).

Vol. IVA.6 *Morality and Public Life in a Time of Change: Bulgarian Philosophical Studies, I,*
V. Prodanov, M. Stoyanova,
ISBN 1-56518-054-2 (cloth); ISBN 1-56518-055-0 (paper).

Vol. IVA.7 *Knowledge and Morality: Georgian PhilosophicalStudies, 1,*
N.V. Chavchavadze, G. Nodia, P. Peachey,
ISBN 1-56518-052-6 (cloth); ISBN 1-56518-053-4 (paper).

Vol. IVA.8 *Cultural Heritage and Social Change: Lithuanian Philosophical Studies, I,*
Bronius Kuzmickas and Aleksandr Dobrynin,
ISBN 1-56518-038-0 (cloth); ISBN 1-56518-039-9 (paper).

Vol. IVA.9 *National, Cultural and Ethnic Identities: Harmony beyond Conflict: Czech Philosophical Studies, IV*
Jaroslav Hroch, David Hollan, George F. McLean
ISBN 1-56518-113-1 (paper).

Vol. IVA.10 *Models of Identities in Postcommunist Societies: Yugoslav Philosophical Studies, I*
Zagorka Golubovic and George F. McLean
ISBN 1-56518-121-1 (paper).

Vol. IVA.11 *Interests and Values: The Spirit of Venture in a Time of Change: Slovak Philosophical Studies, II*
Tibor Pichler and Jana Gasparikova
ISBN 1-56518-125-5 (paper).

Vol. IVA.12 *Creating Democratic Societies: Values and Norms; Bulgarian Philosophical Studies, II*
Plamen Makariev, Andrew M. Blasko, Asen Davidov
ISBN 1-56518-131-X (paper).

Vol. IVA.14 *Values and Education in Romania Today; Romanian Philosophical Studies, I*
Marin Calin and Magdalena Dumitrana
ISBN 1-56518-133-4 (paper).

Vol. IVA.16 *Culture and Freedom; Romanian Philosophical Studies, III*
Marin Aiftinica
ISBN 1-56518-136-0 (paper).

Vol. IVA.17 *Lithuanian Philosophy; Persons and Ideas Lithuanian Philosophical Studies, II*
Jurate Baranova
ISBN 1-56518-1379 (paper).

Vol. IVA.18 *Human Dignity: Values and Justice; Czech Philosophical Studies, III*
Miloslav Bednar

ISBN 1-56518-1409 (paper).

## Series V. Latin America

Vol. V.1 *The Social Context and Values: Perspectives of the Americas,*
O. Pegoraro,
ISBN 0-8191-7354-1 (cloth); ISBN 0-8191-7355-x (paper).

Vol. V.2 *Culture, Human Rights and Peace in Central America,*
Raul Molina, Timothy Ready,
ISBN 0-8191-7356-8 (cloth); ISBN 0-8191-7357-6 (paper).

Vol V.3 *El Cristianismo Aymara: Inculturacion o culturizacion?,*
Luis Jolicoeur
ISBN 1-56518-104-2 (paper).

Vol. V.4 *Love as theFoundation of Moral Education and Character Development*
Luis Ugalde, Nicolas Barros, George F. McLean
ISBN 1-56518-080-1 (paper).

Vol. V.5 *Human Rights, Solidarity and Subsidiarity: Essays towards a Social Ontology*
Carlos E. A. Maldonado
ISBN 1-56518-110-7 (paper).

# FOUNDATIONS OF MORAL EDUCATION AND CHARACTER DEVELOPMENT

## Series VI. Foundations of Moral Education

Vol. VI.1 *Philosophical Foundations for Moral Education and Character Development: Act and Agent,*
G. McLean, F. Ellrod,
ISBN 1-56518-001-1 (cloth); ISBN 1-56518-000-3 (paper).

Vol. VI.2 *Psychological Foundations for Moral Education and Character Development: An Integrated Theory of Moral Development,*
R. Knowles,
ISBN 1-56518-003-8 (cloth); ISBN 1-56518-002-x (paper).

Vol. VI.3 *Character Development in Schools and Beyond,*
Kevin Ryan, Thomas Lickona,

ISBN 1-56518-058-5 (cloth); ISBN 1-56518-059-3 (paper).

Vol. VI.4 *The Social Context and Values: Perspectives of the Americas,*
O. Pegoraro,
ISBN 0-8191-7354-1 (cloth); ISBN 0-8191-7355-x (paper).

Vol. VI.5 *Chinese Foundations for Moral Education and Character Development,*
Tran van Doan,
ISBN 1-56518-033 (cloth), ISBN 1-56518-032-1 (paper).

## The International Society for Metaphysics

Vol.1 *Person and Nature*
George F. McLean and Hugo Meynell, eds.
ISBN 0-8191-7025-9 (cloth); ISBN 0-8191-7026-7 (paper).

Vol.2 *Person and Society*
George F. McLean and Hugo Meynell, eds.
ISBN 0-8191-6924-2 (cloth); ISBN 0-8191-6925-0 (paper).

Vol.3 *Person and God*
George F. McLean and Hugo Meynell, eds.
ISBN 0-8191-6937-4 (cloth); ISBN 0-8191-6938-2 (paper).

Vol.4 *The Nature of Metaphysical Knowledge*
George F. McLean and Hugo Meynell, eds.
ISBN 0-8191-6926-9 (cloth); ISBN 0-8191-6927-7 (paper).

The series is published and distributed by: The Council for Research in Values and Philosophy, Cardinal Station, P.O. Box 261, Washington, D.C. 20064, Tel./Fax: 202/319-6089; e-mail: cua-rvp@cua.edu; website: http://www.crvp.org

Prices: -- Europe and North America: cloth $45.00; paper $17.50; plus shipping: surface, $3.50 first volume; $1.00 each additional; UPS, $5 first copy; air, $7.20. -- Latin American and Afro-Asian editions: $4.00 per volume; plus shipping: sea, $1.75; air, Latin America $5.70; Afro-Asia: $9.00.